Better Homes and Gardens®

ENCYCLOPEDIA
of
COOKING

Volume 6

Cheese-Fruit Relish, a blend of cottage cheese, grapes, and pistachio nuts, is a modern version of the "curds and whey" Little Miss Muffet ate before her encounter with the spider.

On the cover: Peach-Pecan Mold features "peaches and cream" in a show-off dessert. Pecans add crunch to ice cream mold ringed with peach slices. Serve with peach sauce atop.

BETTER HOMES AND GARDENS BOOKS
NEW YORK • DES MOINES

COTTAGE CHEESE—A white, soft, unripened (fresh) cheese with a slightly acidic, yet delicate flavor.

Although this form of cheese was probably one of the first made, its exact origin is unknown. However, the origin of its name is clear. Because of the simple processing involved, cottage cheese has been made for centuries by homemakers throughout the world in their cottages.

Commercial processing of cottage cheese begins with coagulation of pasteurized skim milk. When firm, the cheese is cut into either large or small cubes, then heated and stirred. The whey (watery part of milk) must be drawn off, and the cubes or curds washed with cold water. This action cleans and firms them. The curds are then salted lightly. Cream is added if cream-style cottage cheese is to be made.

To comply with federal standards, cream-style cottage cheese must have at least four percent milk fat. One tablespoon of cream-style has 18 calories compared to 14 in dry cottage cheese. Both the cream and dry types supply protein, minerals, calcium, and B vitamins to the diet.

Cream-style and dry cottage cheeses are available in supermarkets. The cream-style may also be purchased mixed with chives, fruit, or vegetables. The selection of curd size depends on personal preference. Either large or small curds can be used unless one type is specifically called for as a recipe ingredient.

Because the high moisture content of cottage cheese makes it quite perishable, always purchase it from stores that rotate their stock frequently. Refrigerate the cottage cheese as soon as possible after purchasing, being sure it's tightly covered. Use the cheese within a few days for the best flavor and retention of nutrients.

Cottage cheese can be eaten plain or used as an ingredient. Plain cottage cheese makes a good low-calorie snack or salad. Sugar, spices, and fresh, crisp vegetables may be added for additional flavor and texture contrast. As an ingredient, this cheese combines well with other foods for dips, appetizers, soups, salads, main dishes, and desserts. Cottage cheese is a basic ingredient in such dishes as lasagne and cheesecake. (See also *Cheese*.)

Dilled Cheese Casserole

  2 tablespoons butter or margarine
  3 tablespoons all-purpose flour
  2 teaspoons prepared mustard
  ½ teaspoon salt
  2 cups milk
  4 ounces sharp process American cheese, shredded (1 cup)
  2 beaten egg yolks
  1 cup macaroni, cooked and drained
  1 cup cream-style cottage cheese
  ½ cup finely chopped dill pickle
  1 cup soft bread crumbs
  2 tablespoons butter or margarine, melted

In saucepan melt the first 2 tablespoons butter; blend in all-purpose flour, prepared mustard, and salt. Add milk. Cook and stir till thickened and bubbly. Add cheese; cook and stir till melted. Stir small amount of hot mixture into egg yolks; return to saucepan. Cook and stir till bubbly; add cooked macaroni.

Combine cream-style cottage cheese and chopped dill pickle. Spread *half* the macaroni mixture in a 10x6x1¾-inch baking dish; top with cottage cheese mixture and remaining macaroni mixture. Combine soft bread crumbs and melted butter; sprinkle atop casserole. Bake at 350° for 30 minutes. Makes 6 servings.

Mock Lasagne Casserole

  1 pound bulk pork sausage
  1 15-ounce can tomato sauce (2 cups)
  ½ teaspoon garlic salt
  ½ teaspoon dried basil, crushed
  ½ teaspoon pepper
  ½ cup water
  1 7-ounce package macaroni, cooked and drained
  1½ cups cream-style cottage cheese
  6 ounces process American cheese, shredded (1½ cups)

Brown the meat; drain off fat. Add tomato sauce, garlic salt, basil, pepper and water. Cover; simmer 15 minutes, stirring occasionally. In a 2-quart casserole layer *half* each macaroni, cottage cheese, shredded cheese, and meat sauce. Repeat layers. Bake at 375° for 30 minutes. Makes 6 to 8 servings.

Potato-Cottage Bake

      4 medium potatoes, peeled and
          cooked
      1 cup cream-style cottage cheese
      1 egg
      1 teaspoon salt
          Dash pepper
      2 tablespoons snipped parsley
      1 tablespoon butter or margarine

With electric mixer beat potatoes, cottage cheese, egg, salt, and pepper till nearly smooth. Stir in parsley. Turn into well-greased 1-quart casserole. Dot with butter; sprinkle with paprika, if desired. Bake, uncovered, at 350° for 35 minutes. Makes 6 to 8 servings.

Cheese-Fruit Relish

      1 16-ounce carton large curd
          cream-style cottage cheese,
          drained
      1 cup halved seedless green
          grapes
      2 tablespoons coarsely chopped
          pistachio nuts
      ⅓ cup mayonnaise or salad
          dressing
      ¼ teaspoon salt

Combine all ingredients; mix together lightly. Chill. Serve in relish dish or spoon into lettuce cup placed in the center of a fruit platter. Makes about 2⅔ cups.

Cottage Cheese Slaw

      ½ cup cream-style cottage cheese
      ½ cup mayonnaise or salad
          dressing
      2 tablespoons vinegar
      ½ teaspoon caraway seed
      ½ teaspoon onion juice
      ¼ teaspoon Worcestershire sauce
      8 cups shredded cabbage, chilled

Blend together cottage cheese, mayonnaise, vinegar, caraway, onion juice, and Worcestershire sauce. (For stronger caraway flavor, chill mixture several hours.) Just before serving, toss dressing with cabbage. Serves 8 to 10.

Berry-Patch Salad

      2 medium cantaloupes, chilled
      1 12-ounce carton cream-style
          cottage cheese
      1 8¾-ounce can pineapple tidbits,
          chilled and drained
          • • •
      ½ cup hulled and halved fresh
          strawberries
      ½ cup fresh red raspberries

Cut cantaloupes in half crosswise; remove seeds. Combine cottage cheese and pineapple. Spoon into melon halves. Top with strawberries and raspberries. Serves 4.

Lemon Cheesecake

          Crumb crust
      1 cup sugar
      2 envelopes unflavored gelatin
      ¼ teaspoon salt
      1 6-ounce can evaporated milk
      2 beaten egg yolks
      1 teaspoon grated lemon peel
          • • •
      2 12-ounce cartons cream-style
          cottage cheese, sieved
      2 tablespoons lemon juice
      1 teaspoon vanilla
          • • •
      2 egg whites
      1 cup whipping cream

Make *Crumb Crust:* Combine 1 cup zwieback crumbs, ¼ cup sugar, ¾ teaspoon ground cinnamon, ¼ teaspoon ground nutmeg, and ¼ cup butter, melted. Mix till crumbly. Reserve ¼ cup; press remainder on bottom and sides of buttered 9-inch springform pan. Chill.

In a saucepan, combine ¾ *cup* sugar, gelatin, and salt. Stir in evaporated milk, then egg yolks. Cook and stir over low heat till gelatin dissolves. Add lemon peel; cool at room temperature for 30 minutes. Stir in cottage cheese, lemon juice, and vanilla. Chill, stirring occasionally, till mixture mounds. Beat egg whites to soft peaks; gradually add ¼ cup sugar, beating to stiff peaks. Whip cream; fold egg whites and cream into gelatin mixture. Pour into chilled crust; sprinkle with reserved crumbs. Chill overnight. Serves 8.

Chilled Tomato-Cheese Soup

    1 10¾-ounce can condensed cream
        of tomato soup
    2 cups light cream
    1 teaspoon prepared horseradish
    1 teaspoon lemon juice
        Bottled hot pepper sauce
    ½ cup cream-style cottage cheese

Combine tomato soup, cream, horseradish, lemon juice, and a few dashes hot pepper sauce. Beat till well blended. Stir in cottage cheese, ½ teaspoon salt, and dash pepper; chill. Ladle into chilled bowls; sprinkle with chopped onion tops or chives, if desired. Serves 4 to 6.

COTTAGE FRIED POTATOES—Boiled potatoes which are sliced, then fried till crisp. They are also called home fries.

Cottage Fries

Cook potatoes in jackets; peel. Slice or dice. Fry in hot fat till brown and crisp, turning frequently. Season with salt and pepper.

COTTAGE PUDDING—A pudding of plain cake topped with a sauce. It usually consists of yellow cake covered with a fruit or hard sauce. (See also *Dessert*.)

Top warm cake, full of mincemeat and dates, with fluffy vanilla sauce and serve immediately. Mincemeat fans will enjoy Mince Cottage Pudding the year-round for dessert or snacks.

Mince Cottage Pudding

½ cup boiling water
½ cup finely snipped pitted dates
½ cup butter or margarine
½ cup brown sugar
2 eggs
2 cups prepared mincemeat
2¼ cups sifted all-purpose flour
3 teaspoons baking powder
1 teaspoon salt
¼ teaspoon ground nutmeg
¼ cup chopped nuts
Vanilla Sauce

Pour water over dates; cool. Cream butter and sugar till light. Add eggs, one at a time, beating well after each. Add mincemeat and dates to creamed mixture. Sift flour, baking powder, salt, and nutmeg together; mix with creamed mixture just till blended. Stir in nuts. Pour into greased and floured 13x9x2-inch baking dish. Bake at 350° till done, about 35 to 40 minutes. Cut into squares. Serve warm with Vanilla Sauce. Makes 12 servings.

Vanilla Sauce: Beat 3 egg yolks with ¾ cup sifted confectioners' sugar, 1 teaspoon vanilla, and dash salt till thick and yellow. Whip 1 cup whipping cream; fold whipped cream into sauce. Chill. Stir before serving.

Cottage Pudding

½ cup shortening
¾ cup sugar
1 egg
¼ teaspoon lemon extract
1¾ cups sifted all-purpose flour
2½ teaspoons baking powder
½ teaspoon salt
⅔ cup milk
• • •
½ cup sugar
4 teaspoons cornstarch
Dash ground nutmeg
2 beaten egg yolks
2 tablespoons butter or margarine
½ teaspoon grated lemon peel
2 tablespoons lemon juice

Cream together shortening and the ¾ cup sugar; add egg and lemon extract. Beat well. Sift together flour, baking powder, and salt.

Add dry ingredients to creamed mixture alternately with milk, beating after each addition. Bake in lightly greased and floured 9x9x2-inch baking pan at 350° till cake tests done, about 40 to 45 minutes.

Meanwhile, mix the ½ cup sugar, cornstarch, dash salt, and nutmeg in saucepan. Gradually stir in 1 cup water. Cook and stir over low heat till thickened and bubbly. Stir a little hot mixture into beaten egg yolks; return to hot mixture. Cook and stir 1 minute. Remove from heat. Add butter, lemon peel, and lemon juice; blend. Serve sauce over warm cake.

COTTONSEED OIL—A clear, yellow oil with a nutlike odor extracted from the seed of cotton plants. After the oil has been removed from the seed, it must be refined. This process yields a pure, bland oil.

Cottonseed oil is used to make shortening, margarine, salad oil, salad dressing, and mayonnaise. It can also be used as a preservative, especially in canning fish.

Salad oils are available as blends of several oils or as a pure cottonseed oil. Both types are suitable for making salad dressings, panfrying, and deep-fat frying. (See *Fat, Oil* for additional information.)

Carve country-style hams by slicing either lengthwise or across the grain. Each slice should be paper-thin for flavor is very rich.

COULIS *(ku' li)* — A thick sauce or soup made from the juices which come from meat, fish, or poultry during cooking. These are strained and thickened to make the coulis. It can also be made with a meat or fish purée rather than the juice.

COUMARIN *(kōō' muh rin)* — White crystals which have a vanillalike odor and a burning taste. The substance is extracted from the tonka bean and other plants or made synthetically. Coumarin is used to make imitation vanilla and perfume.

COUNTRY-STYLE HAM — Specially cured and aged hams. Country-style hams are part of the Southern tradition and were developed by early settlers to keep during the hot summer months without refrigeration. They are processed in much the same way as Smithfield and Virginia-style hams with curing, smoking, and hanging.

Country-style hams need slow cooking. They must be scrubbed or trimmed, soaked, and simmered before browning in the oven and glazing. (See also *Ham.*)

COUPE *(kōōp)* — 1. A dessert made with ice cream. 2. A stemmed glass with a wide, deep bowl. 3. A rimless plate.

A coupe dessert resembles a sundae or a parfait. Toppings of a sauce, fruit, brandy, liqueur, or whipped cream are mixed with the ice cream, poured over it, or arranged in alternate layers. However, these desserts are assembled in a coupe-type glass rather than the tall parfait or sundae dish. Garnishing with candied flowers, candied fruit, or chopped nuts completes the fancy dessert or refreshment. (See *Dessert, Ice Cream* for additional information.)

Cranberry-Marshmallow Freeze

Pour marshmallow creme over top for coupe—

    1 16-ounce can whole cranberry
        sauce
    1 7-ounce jar marshmallow creme
            • • •
    ½ cup whipping cream
    1 tablespoon lemon juice
        Marshmallow creme

In small mixer bowl, beat cranberry sauce into marshmallow creme. Turn into 3-cup refrigerator tray and freeze till firm. Whip cream. Remove frozen mixture to chilled mixer bowl and break into chunks. Add lemon juice and beat till fluffy. Fold in whipped cream. Return to tray; freeze firm. Makes 1 quart.

Serve in coupe-type glasses topped with additional marshmallow creme.

Cinnamon-Berry Coupe

    1 teaspoon ground cinnamon
    1 quart vanilla ice cream
    1 pint fresh strawberries,
        hulled and sliced
    6 tablespoons sugar
    1 teaspoon grated orange peel
    ½ teaspoon grated lemon peel
    2 tablespoons orange juice
    2 teaspoons lemon juice
    1 10-ounce package frozen rasp-
        berries, thawed
    4 teaspoons cornstarch

Stir cinnamon into ice cream; freeze till firm in refrigerator tray. Combine sliced strawberries, *3 tablespoons* sugar, orange and lemon peel, and orange and lemon juices; chill. Sieve raspberries with syrup.

In saucepan, combine remaining sugar and cornstarch. Add raspberry purée; cook and stir till thickened and bubbly. Remove from heat; add strawberry mixture. Chill.

To serve, alternately layer cinnamon ice cream and berry mixture into coupe-type glasses, ending with ice cream. Serve immediately or return to freezer. Makes 6 servings.

COURT BOUILLON — A broth used in place of water to poach fish or vegetables. The broth consists of onion, carrot, herbs, seasonings, and water or wine, simmered and strained. The liquid can be used, not only for cooking fish and vegetables, but also in making soup and stock.

COUSCOUS — A North African dish containing cracked wheat. (See also *Wheat.*)

COWPEA — An edible bean also known as black-eyed pea. (See also *Black-Eyed Pea.*)

CRAB—A shellfish prized for its delicate, sweet meat. The crab has a flat body shaped in an oval or triangle, five pairs of legs, and a hard shell. A tail which folds up under the body distinguishes it from lobster and shrimp. One of the most unusual characteristics of the crab is its method of locomotion. These active creatures run and crawl sideways.

Crabs are found in salt water and sometimes in fresh water. Primarily, they live in shallow bays, sounds, and mouths of rivers along the Atlantic, Gulf, and Pacific coasts. Only occasionally are they found in the open sea.

The life cycle of a crab begins as a tiny egg. When the egg hatches, the baby measures only 1/25 of an inch and looks like a question mark. As it grows, the crab sheds its shell or "molts" many times. Each time the crab molts, it increases about a third in size. Full maturity is reached and molting ceases after 12 to 14 months. If not caught, a crab may live to three years of age, but few surpass this age.

Crabs are captured with pots, with wire traps on the bottom of a bay, or with baited lines. Often, in winter, crabs are dredged from the floor of a bay where they are hibernating. Once caught, these crabs are kept alive until time for cooking either by the consumer or processing plant. Live crabs, packed in seaweed and kept cold, are flown to markets all over the United States in limited quantities.

The majority of crabs that are caught are sent to processing plants. They are kept alive under carefully controlled temperatures until time for processing. Within seconds of being killed, the crabs are eviscerated and cooked. Immediately, the flesh is extracted or sections which remain in the shell, such as claws, are prepared. Then the meat is packaged, frozen, or canned and ready for market.

Nutritional value: Crab meat is a good source of protein and contains some minerals and B vitamins. If the crab meat is cooked by steaming, its meat will also have vitamin A. Each ½-cup serving of crab meat averages approximately 90 calories. One average serving of fried soft shell crab will contain 185 calories.

Types of crab: There are countless types of crabs inhabiting the American coastal waters. The most familiar are the blue, Dungeness, king, and rock crabs because they are the ones caught and marketed in the largest numbers. These four have the following characteristics and features.

Blue crabs from the middle and south Atlantic and Gulf coasts are an olive green in color. Only the tops of the claws have a blue coloring, despite the name. These crabs weigh from ¼ to 1 pound.

Dungeness crabs are caught along the Pacific coast from Monterey Bay north to Alaska. They are reddish in color and weigh from 1½ to 3½ pounds. The Dungeness meat, rich and distinctive in flavor, is composed of short, tender fibers.

King crabs from Alaska are large, weighing from 6 to 24 pounds, and measuring as much as six feet in length. Long, coarse fibers make up the white, tender meat.

Rock crabs are native to both the New England and California coasts. They are small, weighing only ⅓ to ½ pound, and have brownish colored meat.

Other types of crabs include the buster, stone, hermit, fiddler, robber-palm, spider, and shore. These are found in various regions and yield good meat.

Soft-shell crabs are not a type of crab, but rather a crab which has just shed its hard shell and has not yet grown another.

How to select: A large selection of live crabs and fresh, frozen, and canned crab meat is available in American markets.

Live crabs and fresh crab meat, although available primarily near the coasts, are flown to other sections of the country. Live crabs are usually chilled and packed in seaweed. Select those which are active and have a fresh sea smell. Fresh meat is more common on the markets than is live crab. This meat has been cooked, picked from the shell, and chilled.

Toss this salad at the table

Bring Crab-Artichoke Luncheon Salad to→ the table arranged in an attractive design. Top with the creamy salad dressing and toss.

Frozen crab meat comes in several forms. It may be cooked or uncooked, in the shell or picked from the shell. Packages of parts, such as legs or cocktail crab claws, are also available.

Pasteurized crab meat is sold in cans. This is cooked and ready to eat. Be sure to refrigerate until ready to use.

Canned crab meat is also available. The types available are lump, flake, lump and flake, or claw. Lump meat consists of choice nuggets of white meat from the body. This style is attractive in cocktails and salads. Flaked meat consists of small pieces from the body that are good for casseroles and dips. A lump and flake combination is used for salads, sandwiches, and casseroles. The brownish claw meat does not look as attractive as other forms, but is quite flavorful. It is also cheaper than other forms of crab meat.

The various forms of crab meat are usually interchangeable in recipes. Selection depends on availability, personal preference, cost, and the use intended.

Buy one medium or two small crabs for each person if served whole. Four pounds of crabs with shells will yield about one pound of meat. An average serving per person is about one-fourth pound.

How to store: Live crabs should be cooked immediately. Keep the meat iced or refrigerated if it will be used in one or two days. To prolong storage time, cooked crab meat can be kept frozen for one month.

How to prepare: Canned crab meat requires little preparation. Simply drain and remove bits of cartilage and shell from the meat. Frozen crab meat should be thawed in its original wrap in the refrigerator. Boil or steam commercially frozen meat if it has not been cooked.

Live crabs are cooked in much the same way as are lobsters. They should be alive until the moment of cooking to insure freshness and quality. Crabs can be killed just before cooking or plunged into boiling water—a quick and easy method. Boil crabs about eight minutes per pound or steam about 30 minutes.

To open cooked crabs, crack the shell with a mallet. Then, pull off the back, remove the gills, and break the body in half. Remove the "butter" substance and save for soup or dressing, if desired. Rinse with cold water and pick out the body and claw meat with a nut picker.

Crab meat can be eaten with melted butter or used in hot or cold salads, dips, sandwiches, appetizers, cocktails, and casseroles. (See also *Shellfish*.)

Hot Crab Cocktail Spread

Thoroughly combine one 8-ounce package cream cheese, 1 tablespoon milk, and 2 teaspoons Worcestershire sauce. Add 2 tablespoons chopped green onion and one 7½-ounce can crab meat, drained, flaked, and cartilage removed. Turn into greased 8-inch pie plate. Top with 2 tablespoons toasted slivered almonds. Bake at 350° for 15 minutes. Keep spread warm while serving. Spread on crackers.

Crab Supper Pie

    1 cup shredded natural Swiss
        cheese (4 ounces)
    1 *unbaked* 9-inch pastry shell
    1 7½-ounce can crab meat, drained,
        flaked, and cartilage removed
    2 green onions, sliced (with tops)
    3 beaten eggs
    1 cup light cream
    ½ teaspoon grated lemon peel
    ¼ teaspoon dry mustard
        Dash mace
    ¼ cup sliced almonds

Sprinkle cheese evenly over bottom of pastry shell. Top with crab meat; sprinkle with green onion. Combine eggs, light cream, ½ teaspoon salt, lemon peel, dry mustard, and mace. Pour over crab meat. Top with sliced almonds. Bake at 325° till set, about 45 minutes. Remove from oven and let stand 10 minutes before slicing and serving. Makes 6 servings.

A version of Quiche Lorraine

Add variety to family meals or impress company with Crab Supper Pie, a blend of mildly seasoned cheese, cream, and crab meat.

Deviled Crab Meat Imperial

¼ cup butter or margarine
¼ cup minced green pepper
¼ cup minced onion
¼ cup minced mushrooms
2 tablespoons minced pimiento
1 tablespoon chopped shallots
2 tablespoons all-purpose flour
2 cups light cream
. . .
1 teaspoon salt
Dash pepper
½ teaspoon dry mustard
1 teaspoon Worcestershire sauce
2½ cups flaked crab meat
2½ cups dry white bread crumbs
1 cup hollandaise sauce

Melt butter in skillet. Add green pepper, onion, and mushrooms; cook till tender. Blend in pimiento, shallots, and flour. Add cream and simmer 5 minutes, stirring constantly. Stir in salt, pepper, dry mustard, Worcestershire sauce, crab meat, and *2 cups* bread crumbs (mixture will be thick). Form into 8 balls. Roll balls in remaining crumbs; place in 8 individual baking dishes. Bake at 350° for 15 to 20 minutes. Remove from oven; top each with 2 tablespoons hollandaise sauce. Brown under broiler for about 1 minute. Serve hot. Makes 8 servings.

Crab-Stuffed Mushrooms

3 dozen large, whole, fresh
    mushrooms
1 7½-ounce can crab meat, drained,
    flaked, and cartilage removed
1 tablespoon snipped parsley
1 tablespoon chopped pimiento
1 teaspoon chopped capers
. . .
¼ teaspoon dry mustard
½ cup mayonnaise or salad dressing

Wash and dry mushrooms. With a sharp knife remove stems from mushrooms. (Save stems for use in another recipe.) Combine crab meat, parsley, pimiento, and capers. Blend dry mustard into mayonnaise, toss with crab mixture. Fill each mushroom crown with about 2 tablespoons crab mixture. Bake at 375° till hot, about 8 to 10 minutes. Makes 36 appetizers.

Crab Meat Newberg

6 tablespoons butter
2 tablespoons all-purpose flour
1½ cups light cream
3 beaten egg yolks
. . .
1 cup flaked, cooked crab meat
3 tablespoons dry white wine
2 tablespoons lemon juice
¼ teaspoon salt
    Paprika
    Pastry Petal Cups

Melt butter in skillet; blend in flour. Add cream all at once. Cook, stirring constantly, till sauce thickens and bubbles.

Stir small amount of hot mixture into egg yolks; return to hot mixture. Cook, stirring constantly, till thickened. Add crab meat; heat through. Add wine, lemon juice, and salt. Sprinkle with paprika. Serve in Pastry Petal Cups or over toast points. Makes 4 or 5 servings.

Pastry Petal Cups: Make Plain Pastry (See *Pastry*) or use piecrust mix. Roll ⅛ inch thick; cut in 2¼-inch rounds. In each of 5 muffin cups, place one round in bottom and overlap 4 rounds on sides; press together. Prick bottoms and sides with a fork. Bake at 450° for 10 to 12 minutes. Cool. A recipe that calls for 1½ cups flour will make 5 pastry cups.

Crab Sandwich Broil

1 7½-ounce can crab meat, drained,
    flaked, and cartilage removed
½ cup chopped unpeeled apple
¼ cup chopped celery
½ cup mayonnaise
1 tablespoon lemon juice
. . .
3 hamburger buns, split
3 tablespoons butter or margarine,
    softened
6 slices sharp process American
    cheese

Combine first 5 ingredients. Toast buns and spread with butter; top each half with ⅓ cup crab mixture. Broil 4 inches from heat for 3 to 4 minutes. Top each with slice of cheese; broil till cheese is slightly melted, about 1 to 2 minutes. Makes 6 servings.

King Crab Crown

    1 envelope unflavored gelatin
    3 tablespoons cold water
    2 tablespoons mayonnaise or salad
       dressing
         • • •
    ¼ cup lemon juice
    2 tablespoons finely snipped
       parsley
    4 teaspoons finely snipped chives
    1 tablespoon prepared mustard
    ¼ teaspoon salt
       Dash pepper
    1 7½-ounce can crab meat, drained,
       flaked, and cartilage removed
    1 cup whipping cream
       Unpeeled cucumber slices cut ¼
       inch thick (optional)
       Lemon slices

Soften gelatin in cold water; dissolve over hot water. Stir gelatin into mayonnaise. Blend in lemon juice, parsley, chives, mustard, salt, and pepper. Fold in crab meat. Whip cream; fold into salad. Turn salad into 3½-cup mold. Chill till firm, at least 2 hours. Unmold on chilled platter; garnish with cucumber and lemon slices. Makes 6 servings.

Crab-Artichoke Luncheon Salad

    Salad greens, torn in bite-sized
       pieces (6 cups)
  1½ pounds frozen king crab legs,
       thawed and shelled, *or* 1 6-
       ounce package frozen crab meat,
       thawed, *or* 1 7½-ounce can crab
       meat, drained, and cartilage
       removed
    1 9-ounce package frozen artichoke
       hearts, cooked, drained, and
       chilled
    2 hard-cooked eggs, chopped
       Creamy Salad Dressing

In salad bowl, combine greens. Top with crab meat, artichokes, and eggs. Just before serving toss with dressing. Serves 4 to 6.

Creamy Salad Dressing: Whip ½ cup whipping cream. Combine whipped cream, 1 cup mayonnaise, ¼ cup catsup *or* chili sauce, 2 teaspoons lemon juice, and salt to taste. Chill.

Crab-Tomato Aspic

Soften 2 envelopes unflavored gelatin in ½ cup condensed beef broth. Combine 3 cups tomato juice, 2 slices onion, 2 bay leaves, and ¼ teaspoon celery salt; bring to boiling. Remove onion and bay leaves. Add softened gelatin; stir till dissolved. Add ½ cup condensed beef broth and 2 tablespoons lemon juice. Chill mixture till partially set.

Fold 1 cup chopped celery and one 7½-ounce can crab meat, drained, flaked, and cartilage removed, into gelatin mixture. Turn into 5½-cup mold; chill till firm. Unmold; garnish with hard cooked egg wedges and lettuce in center and around sides of mold. Serves 6.

Crack king crab legs and pick out the sweet, white meat for use in cocktails and salads, such as Crab-Artichoke Luncheon Salad.

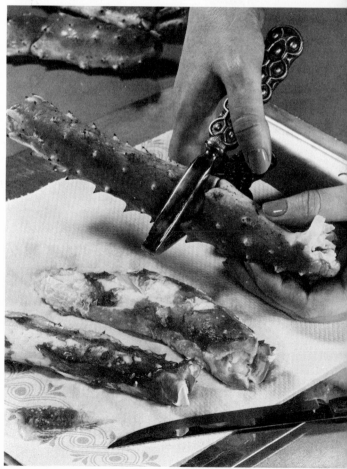

Garnishing meats with crab apples or apple rings gives a spicy, apple flavor plus a bright, colorful accent to the whole meal.

CRAB APPLE—A small, exceptionally tart variety of apple. These apples are 1½ inches in diameter and red in color. A crab apple yields 70 calories but any syrup added will increase the count.

Fresh crab apples are available in the fall, while canned crab apples can be purchased throughout the year. Those in cans or jars are usually packed in a spicy syrup with the stems still attached for a more attractive appearance.

Use crab apples for making jelly, preserves, sauces, and relishes or for an accompaniment with meat. (See also *Apple*.)

Crab Apple Glaze

Colorful glaze and garnish—

Drain one 27-ounce jar spiced whole crab apples, reserving ½ cup syrup. Combine reserved syrup and 1 cup brown sugar in small saucepan; heat and stir till boiling.

Brush syrup glaze on each side of ham slice during last few minutes of boiling. *Or*, brush on broiler-fryer chicken halves several times during last 10 to 15 minutes of broiling. Add crab apples to remaining syrup in saucepan and heat through. Pass warm crab apples with meat or arrange on serving platter.

CRAB BOIL—A blend of spices also called shrimp spice. (See also *Shrimp Spice*.)

CRAB LOUIS—An elaborate main-dish salad. It consists of a bed of lettuce, lumps of crab meat, wedges of hard-cooked eggs, ripe olives, and tomato quarters. A Louis dressing made of mayonnaise, chili sauce, and lemon tops the salad.

This salad was supposedly created on the Pacific coast in 1914 and has been enjoyed throughout the country ever since.

Crab Louis

Substitute shrimp or lobster for a variation—

4 Bibb lettuce cups
8 cups shredded lettuce
   (1 large head)
2 to 3 cups cooked crab meat *or*
   2 7½-ounce cans crab meat,
   chilled and drained

• • •

2 large tomatoes, cut in wedges
2 hard-cooked eggs, sliced
   Louis Dressing
   Pitted ripe olives

Line 4 salad plates with Bibb lettuce cups. Place shredded lettuce atop cups. If necessary, remove cartilage from crab meat. Reserve claw meat; leave remainder in chunks and arrange atop shredded lettuce.

Circle meat with tomato and egg. Sprinkle with salt. Top with claw meat. Pour ¼ cup Louis Dressing atop each salad. Garnish with pitted ripe olives. Pass remaining dressing. Makes 4 servings.

Louis Dressing: Whip ¼ cup whipping cream. Fold 1 cup mayonnaise or salad dressing, ¼ cup chili sauce, ¼ cup chopped green pepper, 2 tablespoons sliced green onion with tops, and 1 teaspoon lemon juice into the whipped cream. Season to taste with salt and pepper; chill.

Salad royalty

Crab Louis, a combination of delicate crab →
meat and tangy dressing, served with bread-
sticks makes a spectacular luncheon menu.

CRACKER—A thin, dry, crisp baked product available in a wide range of sizes and shapes as well as an assortment of flavors. In England, crackers are known as biscuits even though baking powder biscuits also retain this same name.

The simplest cracker recipes are a mixture of flour, water or milk, salt, and usually a leavener such as baking powder. Butter is often added to produce a less crumbly product. The dough is rolled thin, cut, and baked till dry and crisp.

Most of the crackers available in the United States are baked commercially. An increasing array of shapes—square, round, oblong, or fancy—and flavors—plain, salted, seeded, seasoned, sweetened, or unsweetened—line the grocery shelves. There's at least one kind of cracker to please every taste.

The manufactured crackers are carefully packaged to ensure crispness. So that this freshness will be retained, be sure to open each package carefully. Unfold the inner wrap so it can be refolded, thus keeping out atmospheric moisture. If the package is accidentally torn, store the crackers in an airtight container.

However, crackers that become limp need not be thrown away. Crisping is easily achieved by spreading the crackers on a cookie sheet and heating them for a few minutes in a slow oven.

Varieties of crackers enhance menus and function as cooking agents, too. Either a single type or an assortment of the unsweetened varieties are excellent for appetizer or in-between-meal nibblers accompanied by dips, dunks, or cheeses. Their compatibility with salads and soups has long been recognized. Sweetened crackers such as graham crackers are favorites with children and adults alike for desserts or snacks. Some dessert crackers are even chocolate-coated for added richness.

Crackers, when used for cooking, are usually crushed or crumbled. One of the main uses of cracker crumbs is as an extender for meat dishes. When used in this way, the dish will yield more servings per pound of meat. At the same time, the flavor and texture from the crackers also will affect that of the final product to which they may be added.

Meat Loaf Supreme

    1 pound ground pork
    1 pound ground beef
    1 cup shredded carrot
    1 cup coarsely crushed saltine
      crackers (22 crackers)
    1 cup dairy sour cream
  ¼ cup chopped onion
    Mushroom Sauce

Combine first 6 ingredients, 1 teaspoon salt, and dash pepper; mix. Press into 9x5x3-inch loaf pan. Bake at 350° about 1½ hours. Let stand 10 minutes; remove from pan. Serve with *Mushroom Sauce:* Dissolve 1 beef bouillon cube, crushed, in drippings from meat loaf. Combine with ½ cup dairy sour cream, 1 tablespoon all-purpose flour, and one 3-ounce can broiled sliced mushrooms, undrained. Heat just to boiling. Makes 8 to 10 servings.

Crumbs made from crackers may serve to bind ingredients together or to thicken a mixture. They are frequently used in casseroles for such purposes. Soups and sauces can be thickened in this manner.

Salmon Scallop

    1 7¾-ounce can salmon, undrained
  ½ cup finely crushed saltine
      crackers (14 crackers)
  ⅓ cup milk
  ¼ cup chopped celery
    2 teaspoons lemon juice
    Dash dried dillweed
    1 tablespoon butter or margarine

Flake salmon with liquid in bowl, removing skin and bones. Stir in dash pepper and remaining ingredients *except* butter. Turn into ½-quart casserole. Dot with butter. Bake at 350° for 35 minutes. Makes 2 servings.

Cracker-crumb piecrusts make versatile variations for main dishes or desserts. If the crust is baked before adding the filling, the resulting piecrust will be a little crisper. Unbaked dessert crumb crusts should be chilled, then filled.

Ham in Cheese Crust

1½ cups finely crushed round
    cheese crackers (about 36)
6 tablespoons butter or margarine,
    melted

. . .

2 beaten eggs
1 6-ounce can evaporated
    milk (⅔ cup)
¼ cup finely chopped onion
¼ cup finely chopped green pepper
1 tablespoon prepared mustard
1 teaspoon prepared horseradish
1 pound ground fully cooked ham

For crust mix cracker crumbs and butter. Reserving 2 tablespoons crumb mixture, press remaining on bottom and sides of 9-inch pie plate. Bake at 350° for 10 minutes.

Meanwhile, in a bowl combine eggs, evaporated milk, chopped onion, chopped green pepper, mustard, and horseradish. Add ham; mix well. Turn into baked crumb crust. Bake at 350° for 35 minutes.

Sprinkle with reserved 2 tablespoons crumb mixture; bake 5 to 10 minutes longer. Let stand 5 minutes before cutting into wedges. If desired, trim top of pie with additional whole round cheese crackers and a few sprigs of fresh parsley. Makes 6 servings.

Cheese cracker crumbs not only form the shell for Ham in Cheese Crust, but they add an attractive garnish to the top. Additional crackers and parsley are added before serving.

S'More Pie

1¼ cups finely crushed graham
    crackers
¼ cup sugar
6 tablespoons butter or margarine,
    melted
2 cups milk
2 slightly beaten egg yolks
1 3- or 3¼-ounce package *regular*
    vanilla pudding mix
1 cup miniature marshmallows
3 ¾-ounce milk chocolate candy
    bars, broken in pieces
2 egg whites
½ teaspoon vanilla
¼ teaspoon cream of tartar
¼ cup sugar

Combine crumbs, the first ¼ cup sugar, and melted butter; mix well. Press firmly on bottom and sides of 9-inch pie plate. Bake at 375° till edges are brown, about 6 to 8 minutes; cool.

Combine milk and egg yolks; gradually add to pudding mix in saucepan. Cook according to package directions. Cover surface of pudding with waxed paper; cool.

Assorted crackers, attractively arranged, make the ideal partner with Chicken Liver-Onion Dip. (See *Dip* for recipe.)

Place marshmallows over crust; top with chocolate pieces. Spoon cooled pudding evenly over chocolate. Beat egg whites with vanilla and cream of tartar till soft peaks form. Gradually add ¼ cup sugar, beating to stiff peaks. Spread atop pie, sealing to edges of crust. Bake at 375° till golden, about 10 to 12 minutes. Cool thoroughly before serving.

Crackers, whole or crushed, also make an attractive and appealing garnish. On casseroles, crumbs may be added just before baking. Garnish desserts with whole or crushed crackers before serving.

Make cracker crumbs in blender

Use your blender to make cracker crumbs in a hurry. Turn blender on and off quickly to regulate desired fineness of crumbs.

Saltine crackers—to make ½ cup of cracker crumbs, place 13 to 14 crackers in blender container. These can be done all at the same time.

Graham crackers—To make ½ cup of Graham cracker crumbs, break 6 to 7 crackers into the blender container.

Oven-Style Turkey Hash

1½ cups coarsely ground cooked
    turkey
1 cup cubed cooked potato
1 6-ounce can evaporated milk
¼ cup finely snipped parsley
¼ cup finely chopped onion
1 teaspoon Worcestershire sauce
½ teaspoon salt
¼ teaspoon ground sage
    • • •
¼ cup finely crushed saltine
    crackers (7 crackers)
1 tablespoon butter, melted

Stir together first 8 ingredients and dash pepper. Turn into lightly greased 1-quart casserole. Toss crumbs and butter together. Sprinkle atop hash. Bake, uncovered, at 350° till heated through, about 30 minutes. Makes 4 servings.

Mushroom Casserole

Serve as a meat accompaniment or over toast for a main dish—

Cook ½ cup chopped onion in ½ cup butter or margarine till crisp-tender. Add two 6-ounce cans mushroom crowns, drained. Cook lightly. Blend in ¼ cup all-purpose flour and ½ teaspoon dried marjoram leaves, crushed. Add one 10½-ounce can condensed beef broth all at once. Cook and stir till mixture is thickened and bubbly. Remove from heat. Stir in 2 tablespoons dry sherry and 2 tablespoons snipped parsley. Pour mixture into 1-quart casserole.

Combine ½ cup coarsely crushed saltine crackers (11 crackers), 2 tablespoons grated Parmesan cheese, and 1 tablespoon melted butter or margarine. Sprinkle over top of casserole. Bake at 375° till mixture is hot and bubbly, about 15 minutes. Makes 6 servings.

As an outside coating, cracker crumbs add an interesting texture and flavor. Try coating fried and baked foods, such as meatballs, croquettes, chicken, or vegetables with crumbs. A double dipping, of course, gives more crunch. Crumbs also make an equally delicious stuffing.

Cracker Stuffing

  1 cup chopped celery
 ¾ cup chopped onion
 ¼ cup butter or margarine
  2 cups coarsely crushed saltine
     crackers (44 crackers)
 ¾ cup milk
  1 slightly beaten egg
  1 tablespoon snipped parsley
  1 teaspoon dried sage leaves,
     crushed
 ¼ teaspoon dried thyme leaves,
     crushed
 ½ teaspoon salt

In medium skillet cook celery and onion in butter till tender but not brown. Moisten crackers with milk; add onion mixture, egg, parsley, dried sage, dried thyme, salt, and dash pepper. Makes 2⅔ cups stuffing or enough to stuff one 3- to 4-pound chicken.

Crush crackers the easy way with a pizza roller, glass, or rolling pin. The plastic bag, fastened securely, corrals the crumbs.

Sesame Chicken

 ⅔ cup finely crushed saltine
     crackers (18 crackers)
 ¼ cup sesame seed, toasted
  1 2½- to 3-pound ready-to-cook
     broiler-fryer chicken, cut up
 ½ 6-ounce can evaporated
     milk (⅓ cup)
 ½ cup butter, melted

Combine crumbs and toasted sesame seed. Dip chicken pieces in evaporated milk, then roll in crumb mixture. Pour melted butter into 11¾x 7½x1¾-inch baking dish. Dip skin side of chicken pieces in butter; turn over and arrange, skin side up, in baking dish. Bake, uncovered, at 375° till done, about 1 hour. Makes 4 servings.

CRACKER MEAL—The commercial name for fine, unsweetened cracker crumbs.

CRACKLING—1. A crisp bit of tissue that remains after fresh pork fat has been rendered into lard. It is especially liked by Southerners. 2. The crunchy, well-browned fat on roast pork.

CRACKLING BREAD—A corn bread in which crisp cracklings are used as shortening.

CRANBERRY—Bright, red, acid berry of several trailing plants of the heath family. The fruit, native to North America—from Newfoundland to North Carolina and as far west as the states of Minnesota and Arkansas—thrives in cool regions of the Northern Hemisphere. The cultivated berries which have also been introduced into Washington, Oregon, and British Columbia are large, ranging in size from ⅓ to ¾ inch in diameter. (The highbush cranberry, is not a member of this botanical family.)

Species different from those in North America are found in parts of the world with similar climates. The European varieties, however, are somewhat smaller in size with berries from ¼ to ⅓ inch in diameter. One of the better-known species is the lingonberry grown in Scandinavia.

Among the first gifts brought to the Pilgrims by friendly Indians were wild cranberries native to the Massachusetts countryside. Besides eating the berries, the Indians used the brightly colored cranberry juice to dye rugs and blankets and the crushed fruit in a poultice.

The name cranberry is a variation of craneberry, given to the fruit because the pale pink blossoms resemble the head of a crane. In addition, cranes were seen enjoying the fruit while wading in the bogs where cranberries grow.

Cultivation of cranberries did not begin until some 200 years after the landing of the Pilgrims in the New World. A very alert New Englander noted that the largest and juiciest berries were on vines covered by sand blown in from the seashore. Thirty years after this observation the first cranberry bog was built—it is still producing berries. Today, cranberries are grown commercially not only in Massachusetts, but also in New Jersey, Wisconsin, Washington, and Oregon. A limited number of cranberries are also grown in Rhode Island, Michigan, and Maine.

Winter salad bowl spectacular

← Cubes of canned cranberry sauce and tiny orange sections glisten amongst crisp greens in a colorful Cran-Mandarin Toss.

Commercially grown cranberries grow on peat soil that has been covered with a layer of sand. The vines are weeded in the spring and pruned in the fall. Re-sanding is necessary every three to four years. Cranberries are picked and marketed in the fall, a season when an early frost is a definite hazard. Weather forecasts are carefully heeded. When there is the prospect of frost, the vines are protected from frost by flooding the bogs.

In the early days, cranberries were picked by hand. Next came the wooden fingered scoops which combed the berries from the vines. Now mechanical pickers have taken over the job, doing the harvesting in a shorter time. There is even a type of water harvesting in which the berries are knocked off the vines onto flooded fields and floated onto conveyers.

Nutritional value: Raw cranberries are relatively low in calories. One cup of berries contains 46 calories, but this increases as sugar or other ingredients are added to temper the natural sourness of the fruit. Thus, one-half cup cranberry sauce prepared at home will contain approximately 178 calories. Cranberries are also sources of iron and vitamin C.

Fresh cranberries: Good quality in fresh berries is indicated by fresh, plump appearance with a high luster and firmness of fruit. The shade of red does not indicate ripeness because each variety of cranberry produces fruit with a slightly different red hue—some light, some dark.

Good berries bounce when dropped; poor berries just roll. Thus, bounce is one of the tests fresh cranberries must pass when being sorted and graded for market or for use by a processor. The homemaker in her kitchen washing cranberries for use in a recipe will also discard berries that are soft or have bruises.

Cranberries are marketed in several forms. During the fall months the berries are available fresh. At other times whole berries may be found in frozen food cases. All year round shoppers will see canned and frozen cranberry products such as sauce, relish, and juice cocktail, packaged alone or in combination with other fruits.

Fresh cranberries lend their cheery color and tart flavor to many dishes. There are tempting relishes to accompany meat and poultry plus fragrant breads, salads, and easy, colorful desserts.

Cranberry Sauce

Use this same basic recipe to prepare either a spoonable sauce or one to serve jellied—

>   2 cups sugar
>   2 cups water
>   1 pound fresh cranberries (4 cups)

Combine sugar and water in large saucepan; stir to dissolve sugar. Heat to boiling; boil 5 minutes. Add cranberries; cook till skins pop, about 5 minutes. Remove from heat. Serve warm or chilled. Makes 4 cups.

To mold, cook longer till a drop jells on cold plate, about 10 minutes. Pour into 4½-cup mold. Chill till firm.

Pass Cranberry-Date Relish, a medley of fruits, nuts, and spices, especially created for enjoyment with the holiday bird.

Celery Cran-Relish

An uncooked accompaniment, sweet yet tangy—

>   1 pound fresh cranberries (4 cups)
>   2 cups coarsely chopped celery
>   1 medium unpeeled apple, cut up
> 1½ cups sugar
>   2 tablespoons lemon juice

Using coarse blade of food chopper, grind the cranberries, celery, and apple. Stir in sugar and lemon juice; chill. Will keep in refrigerator for several weeks. Makes about 4 cups.

Cranberry-Date Relish

Cooked relish that takes only minutes to prepare—

>   1 pound fresh cranberries (4 cups)
>   1 cup sugar
>   1 cup snipped dates
> ½ cup light raisins
>   2 cups water
> ¼ cup vinegar
> ¼ teaspoon ground cinnamon
> ¼ teaspoon ground ginger

In a medium saucepan combine cranberries, sugar, snipped dates, raisins, water, vinegar, cinnamon, and ginger. Bring to boiling point and boil rapidly, uncovered, for about 10 minutes, stirring occasionally. Remove from heat. Chill. Makes 4 cups relish.

Cranberry Waldorf

>   2 cups fresh cranberries
>   3 cups miniature marshmallows
> ¾ cup sugar
>   2 cups diced unpeeled tart apple
> ½ cup seedless green grapes
> ½ cup broken walnuts
> ¼ teaspoon salt
>   1 cup whipping cream

Grind cranberries and combine with marshmallows and sugar. Cover and chill overnight. Add apple, grapes, walnuts, and salt. Whip cream; fold into fruits. Chill. Serve in a large bowl or in individual lettuce cups. Garnish with grapes, if desired. Serves 8 to 10.

Tantalize guests by serving Cranberry Ice when the turkey is being carved. This pretty pink accompaniment is not dessert. Instead, its a refreshing treat with meat or poultry.

Cranberry-Banana Bread

Cream ¼ cup butter and 1 cup sugar. Add 1 egg; beat. Sift 2 cups sifted all-purpose flour, 3 teaspoons baking powder, and ½ teaspoon *each* salt and ground cinnamon. Add alternately with mixture of 1 cup mashed banana, ¼ cup milk, and 1 teaspoon shredded orange peel. Stir in 1½ cups fresh cranberries, ground and drained, and 1 cup chopped pecans. Turn into greased 9x5x3-inch pan; bake at 350° 1 hour.

Cranberry Coleslaw

Combine ¼ cup sliced fresh cranberries, 1 tablespoon honey, and 1 teaspoon celery seed; let stand 15 minutes. Add ¼ cup mayonnaise and 1 teaspoon vinegar; mix. Toss with 3 cups shredded cabbage. Season. Serves 4 to 5.

Cranberry Nut Loaf

Bright flecks of cranberry in every slice—

    3 cups sifted all-purpose flour
    1 cup sugar
    4 teaspoons baking powder
    1 teaspoon salt
    1 beaten egg
 1½ cups milk
    2 tablespoons salad oil
 1 cup coarsely chopped cranberries
    ½ cup chopped nuts

Sift together dry ingredients. Combine egg, milk, and salad oil; add to dry ingredients, stirring just till moistened. Stir in cranberries and nuts. Turn mixture into greased 9x5x3-inch loaf pan. Bake at 350° till done, about 1¼ hours. Remove from pan; cool on rack.

Cranberry Chutney

1 pound fresh cranberries (4 cups)
2¼ cups brown sugar
1 cup light raisins
½ cup coarsely chopped maca-
damia nuts *or* toasted almonds
¼ cup snipped candied ginger
¼ cup lemon juice
2 teaspoons salt
1 teaspoon grated onion
¼ teaspoon ground cloves

In large saucepan combine all ingredients with 1 cup water. Bring to boiling, stirring constantly. Simmer, uncovered, over low heat for 15 minutes, stirring occasionally. Pack in hot scalded jars; seal at once and refrigerate till used. Makes about 5 half pints.

Cranberry-Banana Shortcake

A fruit duet topping tender, rich desserts—

1 cup sugar
2 cups fresh cranberries
2 bananas, sliced
6 individual biscuits *or* short
cakes (see *Biscuit*)

Combine sugar and ½ cup water in saucepan and stir until dissolved. Boil 5 minutes. Add cranberries and cook till skins pop, about 5 minutes. Remove from heat. Stir in banana slices. Serve on biscuits. Top with whipped cream, if desired. Makes 6 servings.

Cranberry-Avocado Mold

2 3-ounce packages raspberry-
flavored gelatin
2 cups boiling water
1 cup fresh cranberries, ground
½ cup sugar
1 avocado, peeled and cubed
¼ cup chopped walnuts

Dissolve gelatin in boiling water; add 1½ cups cold water. Chill till partially set. Combine cranberries, sugar, dash salt, avocado, and nuts; fold into gelatin. Pour into 6½-cup mold; chill till firm. Makes 8 servings.

Cranberry juice cocktail: Its sparkling, clear red color and not-too-sweet flavor make this bottled fruit drink popular as a breakfast beverage or served as an appetizer for a change of pace. The juice is sweetened and vitamin C is usually added during processing. A 5-ounce serving contains about 65 calories.

Because it mixes well with other fruit juices or carbonated beverages, cranberry juice cocktail is an excellent base for fruit punch or mixed drinks served over ice. It may also be used to make a beautiful jelly or to provide the liquid in a glowing molded salad filled with fruit.

Cranberry Jelly

A clear, ruby-red jelly to give away or enjoy at the family holiday feast—

3½ cups cranberry juice cocktail
1 2¼-ounce package powdered
fruit pectin
4 cups sugar
¼ cup lemon juice

In large saucepan or kettle, combine cranberry juice and pectin. Stir over high heat till cranberry mixture comes to full rolling boil. Stir in sugar immediately. Bring to full rolling boil again; boil hard 2 minutes, stirring constantly. Remove from heat; stir in lemon juice. Skim foam off surface. Pour jelly into hot scalded jars. Makes 6 half pints.

Cranberry-Waldorf Mold

2 cups cranberry juice cocktail
1 3-ounce package lemon-flavored
gelatin
• • •
¼ teaspoon salt
1 cup diced unpeeled apple
½ cup chopped celery
¼ cup broken walnuts

Heat *1 cup* cranberry juice cocktail and gelatin over low heat till gelatin is dissolved. Add remaining juice and the salt. Chill till partially set. Stir in apple, celery, and nuts. Pour into 4 to 6 individual molds. Chill firm. Serves 4 to 6.

Cranberry-Tea Punch

    5 tea bags *or* 5 teaspoons
        loose tea
  1/4 teaspoon ground cinnamon
  1/4 teaspoon ground nutmeg
  3/4 cup sugar
    2 cups cranberry juice cocktail
  1/2 cup orange juice
  1/3 cup lemon juice

Steep tea and spices in 2½ cups boiling water 5 minutes. Remove tea. Add sugar; stir till dissolved; cool. Add fruit juices and 1½ cups water. Chill. Serve over ice. Serves 6 to 8.

Ruby Fruit Punch

  1 28-ounce bottle ginger ale,
    chilled
  1 tablespoon lemon juice
    Orange slices
  4 cups cranberry juice cocktail,
    chilled
  1 cup apple juice, chilled

Place chilled ginger ale, lemon juice, and a few orange slices in punch bowl. Slowly add chilled cranberry juice cocktail and chilled apple juice, stirring gently to blend. Add ice cubes. Makes about 16 servings.

Gaily-bobbing orange slices decorate the punch bowl brimming with Ruby Fruit Punch. Another time serve a tea-based cranberry party punch delicately spiced with cinnamon.

Canned jellied and whole cranberry sauce:
Although most often spooned right from
the can to the serving dish, these handy
sauces are very useful as an ingredient.
They are used as basting sauces for hamburgers and pot roasts. Spicy beverages,
tossed and molded salads, quick breads,
such as muffins, and desserts depend upon
these sauces for flavor and color.

Cranberry Ice

A sophisticated partner for the holiday turkey—

    1 16-ounce can jellied cranberry
        sauce
    1 7-ounce bottle lemon-lime
        carbonated beverage

Beat cranberry sauce till smooth. Resting bottom on rim of bowl, slowly pour in lemon-lime
beverage. Mix gently with up-and-down mo-
tion. Pour mixture into 1-quart freezer tray.
Freeze till firm. Break into chunks with wooden
spoon and place in chilled bowl. Beat till fluffy.
Return mixture to freezer tray and freeze till
firm. Makes 1 quart.

Hot Buttered Cranberry Swizzle

    ¾ cup brown sugar
     1 cup water
    ½ teaspoon ground cinnamon
    ½ teaspoon ground allspice
    ½ teaspoon ground cloves
    ¼ teaspoon salt
    ¼ teaspoon ground nutmeg
     2 16-ounce cans jellied cranberry
        sauce
     3 cups water
     4 cups pineapple juice
        Butter or margarine
        Cinnamon sticks

In large saucepan combine brown sugar, the 1
cup water, the ground cinnamon, allspice,
cloves, salt, and nutmeg. Cook over medium
heat till boiling. Add cranberry sauce and beat
till smooth. Slowly stir in the 3 cups water.
Add pineapple juice; simmer, uncovered, about
5 minutes. Serve in mugs. Dot with butter.
Serve with cinnamon sticks. Serves 10 to 12.

Chicken Pecan Salad in Shimmering Cranberry Ring

    2 3-ounce packages lemon-flavored
        gelatin
    ¼ teaspoon salt
    2 cups orange juice
    1 16-ounce can whole cranberry
        sauce
    3 medium peaches, peeled and
        sliced (1½ cups)*
    3 cups cubed cooked chicken
    1 cup diced celery
            •   •   •
    ½ cup mayonnaise
    2 tablespoons salad oil
    1 tablespoon vinegar
    ½ teaspoon salt
    ¼ cup toasted broken pecans

Dissolve gelatin and salt in *1 cup* orange juice
and 1 cup water, heated to boiling. Stir in 1 cup
cold orange juice. Chill till partially set. Stir
in whole cranberry sauce. Pour into 6½-cup
ring mold. Chill till firm.

Reserve a few peach slices for garnish. Cut
up remaining peaches. In large bowl, combine
cut up peaches, chicken, and celery. Blend together mayonnaise, salad oil, vinegar, and salt.
Toss with chicken mixture. Chill. Before serving, fold in nuts. Serve in center of Cranberry
Ring. Garnish with peaches. Makes 6 servings.
*To keep bright color, dip in lemon or orange
juice mixed with a little water.

Cranberry-Apricot Salad

    1 16-ounce jar refrigerated
        fruit salad
    1 16-ounce can jellied cranberry
        sauce, chilled
    1 cup seedless green grapes
    1 22-ounce can apricot pie
        filling
    1 cup miniature marshmallows
    ½ cup chopped pecans

Drain fruit salad thoroughly. Cut cranberry
sauce into ½-inch cubes and add to fruit salad.
Fold in grapes, apricot pie filling, and marshmallows. Chill salad mixture thoroughly, about
4 to 5 hours. Just before serving, stir in the
chopped pecans. Makes 6 to 8 servings.

Cranberry Star Mold practically makes itself when canned whole cranberry sauce and crushed pineapple team up in a do-ahead salad. The garnish is orange and grapefruit sections.

Cranberry Star Mold

   2 3-ounce packages orange-
       flavored gelatin
   1 16-ounce can whole cranberry
       sauce
   1 8¾-ounce can crushed pine-
       apple, undrained
   2 7-ounce bottles ginger ale
       Canned orange and grapefruit
       sections

In saucepan combine gelatin and cranberry sauce. Heat and stir till almost boiling and gelatin is dissolved. Stir in undrained pineapple and ginger ale. When fizzing has stopped, pour into 5½-cup star mold. Chill till set. Unmold.

Garnish with greens and orange and grapefruit sections. If desired, center sections with a few whole cranberries. Serve with mayonnaise or salad dressing. Makes 8 servings.

Cran-Cheese Frosties

   1 16-ounce can jellied cranberry
       sauce
   2 tablespoons lemon juice
   1 3-ounce package cream cheese,
       softened
   ¼ cup mayonnaise or salad
       dressing
   ¼ cup sifted confectioners' sugar
   ¼ cup chopped walnuts
   1 cup whipping cream

Beat cranberry sauce and lemon juice till smooth. Pour into 6 to 8 paper baking cups, filling about ⅓ full or one 4-cup freezer tray. Beat together softened cream cheese, mayonnaise, and confectioners' sugar. Stir in walnuts. Whip cream. Fold whipped cream into cream cheese mixture; spread over cranberry layer. Freeze till firm. Serve on lettuce. Serves 6 to 8.

Cran-Mandarin Toss

   1 envelope creamy French salad
     dressing mix
  ½ teaspoon grated orange peel
   8 cups torn mixed salad greens
   1 11-ounce can mandarin orange
     sections, drained
   1 8-ounce can jellied cranberry
     sauce, chilled and cubed

Prepare salad dressing mix according to package directions, adding orange peel; chill. In large salad bowl toss together greens and mandarin orange sections. Add cranberry sauce cubes to salad and mix gently. Spoon onto salad plates. Pass dressing. Makes 8 servings.

Cranberry Burger Sauce

   1 16-ounce can whole cranberry
     sauce
  ¼ cup finely chopped celery
   1 tablespoon brown sugar
   3 tablespoons Worcestershire
     sauce
   1 tablespoon salad oil

Combine all ingredients. Grill hamburgers a few minutes on each side before basting with sauce. Makes about 2 cups sauce.

Cranberry-Raisin Stuffing

  14 cups soft bread cubes (about
     14 slices bread)
  ¼ cup butter or margarine,
     melted
   1 16-ounce can whole cranberry
     sauce
  ½ cup raisins
  ¼ cup sugar
   1 teaspoon salt
   1 teaspoon lemon juice
  ½ teaspoon ground cinnamon

Toast bread cubes in 300° oven for about 15 minutes; toss with melted butter or margarine. Add cranberry sauce, raisins, sugar, salt, lemon juice, and cinnamon; toss lightly till well mixed. Makes 8 cups stuffing. This amount is enough to stuff a 12-pound turkey.

Cranberry Pot Roast

   2 tablespoons all-purpose flour
   1 teaspoon salt
   1 teaspoon onion salt
  ¼ teaspoon pepper
   1 3- to 4-pound round-bone pot
     roast
   2 tablespoons salad oil
   4 whole cloves
   2 inches stick cinnamon
  ¼ cup water
   1 16-ounce can whole cranberry
     sauce
   1 tablespoon vinegar

Combine flour, salt, onion salt, and pepper; rub onto surfaces of meat (use all of mixture). In Dutch oven slowly brown meat on both sides in oil. Add spices and water. Cover tightly; simmer till tender, about 2½ hours. Add more water if necessary.

    Pour off excess fat. To meat add cranberry sauce, 2 tablespoons water, and vinegar; cover and cook 10 to 15 minutes. Pass sauce with meat. Makes 6 to 8 servings.

Plymouth Cranberry Cake

   1 16-ounce can whole cranberry
     sauce
   2 tablespoons butter or margarine
   1 package 1-layer-size white
     cake mix
  ¼ cup butter or margarine
  ½ cup sifted confectioners' sugar
  ½ cup cold water
 1½ *teaspoons* cornstarch
   1 teaspoon vanilla
  ½ teaspoon vinegar

Break up cranberry sauce in buttered 8¼x1¾-inch round ovenware cake dish, spreading evenly. Dot with 2 tablespoons butter. Prepare cake mix according to package directions; pour over cranberries. Bake at 350° for 35 to 40 minutes. Let stand 10 minutes; invert on plate. Serve warm with *Butter Sauce:* Cream ¼ cup butter. Gradually add confectioners' sugar, creaming till fluffy. In small saucepan, combine cold water and cornstarch; cook and stir till thick and bubbly. Stir into butter mixture. Add vanilla and vinegar. Serve warm.

Cranberry Cheese Pie

1⅓ cups flaked coconut
¼ cup melted butter or margarine
1 8-ounce package cream cheese
½ cup whipping cream
¼ cup sugar
½ teaspoon vanilla
1 16-ounce can whole cranberry
    sauce

Toast coconut in a 350° oven about 10 minutes, stirring often. Combine with butter or margarine. Press into an 8-inch pie plate.

Beat cream cheese till softened. Whip cream till thickened, but not stiff; add sugar and vanilla. Gradually add to cream cheese beating till smooth and creamy. Fold in cranberry sauce. Spoon into crust. Chill until firm.

Cranberry-Cube Muffins

1 8-ounce can jellied cranberry
    sauce
1¾ cups sifted all-purpose flour
¼ cup sugar
2½ teaspoons baking powder
¾ teaspoon salt
1 well-beaten egg
¾ cup milk
⅓ cup salad oil

Cut cranberry sauce into ½-inch cubes; set aside. Sift flour, sugar, baking powder, and salt into a bowl. Make a well in the center. Combine egg, milk, and oil. Add all at once to dry ingredients. Stir quickly, just till dry ingredients are moistened. Fill greased muffin cups ⅓ full. Sprinkle cranberry cubes over batter. Add more batter till muffin cups are ⅔ full. Bake muffins at 400° for about 25 minutes. Makes 12 muffins.

Other cranberry products: The shopper will find cranberries appearing as an ingredient in packaged mixes for quick breads or in a tasty canned or frozen relish to serve with meat and poultry. Cranberry-orange relish is particularly handy to use in perking up a molded gelatin salad or to top canned peach halves as a quick meat accompaniment. (See also *Berry*.)

Cranberry Relish Salad

Thaw one 10-ounce package frozen cranberry-orange relish. Dissolve one 3-ounce package strawberry-flavored gelatin in 1 cup boiling water. Drain one 8¾-ounce can pineapple tidbits reserving the syrup. Add enough water to the syrup to measure ½ cup. Add syrup and relish to gelatin. Chill till partially set. Stir in pineapple and ⅓ cup finely chopped celery. Chill in 4½-cup mold till firm. Serves 6.

CRAPPIE—A freshwater member of the sunfish family, native only to the United States. They are found in Eastern and Midwestern ponds, creeks, lakes, and rivers, especially in the Great Lakes region and the Mississippi River. Both white and black crappies are prized by the sports fisherman because these fish are aggressive fighters even though their average size is only 10 to 12 inches in length.

The flesh of the crappie is tender, white, and flavorful. These fish are excellent for panfrying. (See also *Fish*.)

CRAWDAD—A colloquial name in the United States for crayfish or crawfish.

CRAYFISH, CRAWFISH—Several varieties of shellfish which resemble the lobster but are only distantly related to it. The larger varieties, also known as spiny lobster and rock lobster, are found in Atlantic waters off the southern coast of the United States and in the Caribbean area. Similar types, some growing very large, are found in the Mediterranean and western Pacific.

The small American crayfish is found in fresh water in the Midwest and Pacific states, in particular. The flavor of all varieties resembles that of lobster, and the meat can be used just as lobster would be in sauced dishes. In Sweden boiled crayfish is a popular dish. The French prepare it in a bisque, in a delicious cold mousse, or serve it *au gratin*. (See *Lobster*, *Shellfish* for additional information.)

CRAZY PUDDING—A name given to pudding cakes which look like cake batter when they go into the oven, but create a sauce during baking. (See also *Pudding Cake*.)

CREAM *(noun)* — The fat-rich portion which rises to the top when milk has not been homogenized. This is quite easy to skim off by hand or with a mechanical separator because cream is lighter in weight than milk. The separator removes the cream by centrifugal force and can be adjusted so that cream of any given fat content is produced. The cream is then removed, pasteurized, and may be homogenized.

Cream should always be stored in the refrigerator. Used alone or as a recipe ingredient, cream provides calories and a small amount of vitamin A in the diet.

Calories in cream

The calorie content reflects the percentage of milk fat in the cream. The following table lists the *calories found in 1 tablespoon:*

Half and half......................20
  (10 to 12% fat)

Dairy sour cream..................29
  (not less than 18% fat)

Light cream.......................32
  (not less than 18% fat)

Whipping cream
  Light...........................45
    (30 to 36% fat)
  Heavy...........................52
    (not less than 36% fat)

Pasteurized cream whips, sold in pressurized cans, contain added ingredients such as sugar, flavorings, and stabilizers. Other products resembling cream made with non-milk fats and milk solids are also marketed. In addition, dried or frozen cream substitutes containing no dairy products are available on the market.

There are many uses for cream. It adds richness and flavor to beverages, salads, sauces, and desserts. Light cream, often called table or coffee cream, is used for coffee, fruit, and cereal as well as in cooking. Whipped cream provides volume in numerous desserts. It also serves as an attractive garnish. (See *Half and Half, Light Cream, Sour Cream, Whipping Cream* for additional information.)

Sherried Ice Cream Roll

  4 egg whites
  ½ cup granulated sugar
  4 egg yolks
  ¼ cup granulated sugar
  ½ teaspoon vanilla
  ⅔ cup sifted cake flour
  ¼ cup unsweetened cocoa powder
  1 teaspoon baking powder
  ¼ teaspoon salt
    Confectioners' sugar
    Sherried Ice Cream
    Whipped cream

Beat egg whites till soft peaks form; gradually add the ½ cup granulated sugar. Beat till stiff peaks form. Beat egg yolks till thick and lemon colored; gradually beat in the ¼ cup granulated sugar. Add vanilla. Fold yolks into whites. Sift together flour, cocoa, baking powder, and salt; fold into egg mixture.

Spread batter evenly in greased and lightly floured 15½x10½x1-inch jelly roll pan. Bake at 375° till done, about 10 to 12 minutes.

Immediately loosen sides and turn out on towel sprinkled with sifted confectioners' sugar. Starting at narrow end, roll cake and towel together; cool on rack.

To prepare *Sherried Ice Cream:* Combine 2 cups soft coconut macaroon crumbs (9 macaroons) and ¼ cup dry sherry. Stir into 1 quart vanilla ice cream, softened. Add 1 cup dairy sour cream; mix well. Freeze in freezer tray.

To assemble, stir sherried ice cream to soften. Unroll jelly roll and spread with ice cream. Roll up; wrap in foil. Freeze. Garnish with whipped cream. Serves 10 to 12.

Cream-laden desserts

Whether it is ice cream, whipped cream, or → dairy sour cream, cream adds richness to this display of desserts—Sherried Ice Cream Roll, Pineapple Parfait Cake (see *Ice Cream* for recipe), and Party Pumpkin Pie.

Party Pumpkin Pie

    1 pint vanilla ice cream,
        softened
    1 tablespoon snipped candied
        ginger
    1 *baked* 9-inch pastry shell,
        cooled
    1 cup canned pumpkin
    ½ cup sugar
    ½ teaspoon salt
    ½ teaspoon ground ginger
    ¼ teaspoon ground nutmeg
    1 cup whipping cream
  1½ cups miniature marshmallows

Combine ice cream and candied ginger. Spread in cooled pastry shell. Freeze. Mix pumpkin and next 4 ingredients. Whip cream; fold into pumpkin mixture. Fold in marshmallows. Pile atop ice cream layer; freeze. Garnish with additional whipped cream, if desired.

Gourmet Pork Chops

    6 loin pork chops, about ½
        inch thick
    2 tablespoons all-purpose flour
    1 teaspoon salt
      Dash pepper
    1 10½-ounce can condensed cream
        of mushroom soup
    ¾ cup water
    ½ teaspoon ground ginger
    ¼ teaspoon dried rosemary
        leaves, crushed
    1 3½-ounce can French-fried
        onions
    ½ cup dairy sour cream

Trim excess fat from chops. Heat fat in skillet till about 2 tablespoons melted fat has collected; discard trimmings. Coat chops in mixture of flour, salt, and pepper. Brown in hot fat. Place in 11x7x1½-inch baking pan.

Combine soup, water, ginger, and rosemary; pour over chops. Sprinkle with *half* the onions. Cover; bake at 350° till meat is tender, about 50 minutes. Uncover; sprinkle with remaining onions. Bake, uncovered, 10 minutes more.

Remove meat to platter. Blend sour cream into soup mixture; heat through, *but do not boil.* Pass with meat. Makes 6 servings.

Raspberry Cream Pudding

Thoroughly drain one 10-ounce package frozen raspberries, thawed, reserving syrup. Chill berries. Add water to reserved syrup to make 1½ cups. Combine one 3- or 3¼-ounce package regular vanilla pudding mix with the 1½ cups liquid. Cook and stir over medium heat till mixture comes to boiling. Remove from heat. Cover; chill till thick, about 2 hours.

Beat chilled mixture smooth with rotary beater. Whip ½ cup whipping cream. Fold whipped cream into pudding mixture. Spoon into sherbet glasses; chill about 2 hours.

To serve, wreathe puddings with ¼ cup vanilla wafer crumbs (6 or 7 wafers); top with well-drained raspberries. Makes 4 to 6 servings.

Basic Vanilla Ice Cream

    ¾ cup sugar
    ½ envelope unflavored gelatin
        (1½ teaspoons)
    4 cups light cream
    1 slightly beaten egg
    2 teaspoons vanilla

In saucepan combine sugar and gelatin. Add *2 cups* of the cream. Stir over low heat till gelatin dissolves. Slowly stir small amount of hot mixture into egg; mix well.

Return to hot mixture; cook, stirring constantly, till mixture is slightly thickened, about 1 minute. Remove from heat; chill. Add remaining cream, vanilla, and dash salt. Freeze in ice cream freezer. Makes 1½ quarts.

Strawberry Ice Cream: Prepare Basic Vanilla Ice Cream *except decrease sugar to ½ cup and reduce vanilla to 1 teaspoon.* Crush 4 cups fresh, ripe strawberries; combine with ¾ cup sugar. Stir crushed berries into chilled mixture. Freeze in ice cream freezer.

Peach Ice Cream: Prepare Basic Vanilla Ice Cream *except decrease sugar to ½ cup and reduce vanilla to 1 teaspoon.* Combine 3 cups mashed, fresh peaches; ¾ cup sugar; and ¼ teaspoon almond extract; stir into chilled mixture. Freeze in ice cream freezer.

Cherry Ice Cream: Prepare Basic Vanilla Ice Cream *except reduce vanilla to 1 teaspoon.* To chilled mixture stir in ⅓ cup maraschino cherries, chopped, and 1 tablespoon maraschino cherry juice. Freeze in ice cream freezer.

CREAM *(verb)*—To beat to a light and fluffy consistency. Shortening may be creamed alone or together with sugar until it is very soft and creamy. A mixture may be creamed by using an electric mixer or by rubbing the mixture against the side of a bowl with the back of a spoon.

CREAM CHEESE—Soft, unripened cheese made from light cream. The origin of cream cheese is unclear. Most likely it originated with early nomadic tribesmen who had to contend with the problem of utilizing soured milk. Having a limited food supply, they were reluctant to discard any food, regardless of its freshness. They learned that milk, like meat, was more easily preserved when dried. So, they developed methods for evaporating milk.

One method devised was to allow fresh milk, poured into shallow containers, to sour under the heat of the sun. As part of the moisture was lost in the process, a thick, acid curd was left. The mixture, similar to what is known as yogurt today, could be further dried to obtain "dried cream"—a primitive form of cream cheese. Another method of evaporating the milk consisted of spooning the curd of soured and separated milk into a wicker mold. The curd was then pressed and drained to remove all the whey.

In time, cream replaced milk in the process. It was allowed to dry in a perforated box lined with two loose layers of cheesecloth. After drying, a firm, but spreadable cheese remained.

Cream cheese, like most other cheeses during their initial period of development, was most often consumed in the country or area where it was developed. Thus, cream cheese is referred to as a fresh, country cheese. However, the cream cheese that appears on the market today is mass-produced in large factories many miles from the source of the milk supply.

Cream cheese was first produced in the United States during the 1870s by a dairyman in New York. About ten years later, commercial production of cream cheese began. Today, it is one of the most popular packaged cheeses in the world.

How cream cheese is produced: A standard procedure for making cream cheese has been developed through mass production. The cream is pasteurized in large vats and quickly cooled. Then a starter of lactic acid bacteria is added to develop the desired acidity and obtain a uniform coagulation. Sometimes rennet is used along with the starter. When coagulation occurs, the curd is heated to express the whey and then mechanical separators separate the whey from the cheese.

After the whey is removed, the cheese is salted and packaged in foil or sealed in jars. This finished cheese-form must contain less than 55% moisture and a minimum of 33% milk fat in order to comply with government standards.

Another soft, unripened cheese, Neufchâtel, is similar to cream cheese both in production and in final form. However, Neufchâtel is higher in moisture and lower in milk fat than cream cheese.

Nutritional value: Two tablespoons of cream cheese supplies 105 calories. Since it is made from cream, it provides many of the milk nutrients such as protein, calcium, phosphorus, the B vitamin riboflavin, and vitamin A. However, cream cheese is most often eaten in small quantities; thus, only small amounts of the above mentioned nutrients are present.

How to select: Cream cheese is available at the dairy counter in the supermarket. Unless sealed in jars, it is most often sold in foil-wrapped packages to prevent loss of moisture. The cheese should be white with no yellowing or evidence of leakage. Sometimes cream cheese is whipped, giving it a lighter, fluffier quality.

Soft cream cheese—available in bars and dips.

The soft, creamy texture of cream cheese blends easily with other ingredients in the preparation of ready-to-serve dips and spreads. Having a mild flavor, cream cheese is usually combined with bacon, clams, shrimp, pimientos, olives, chives, onion, horseradish, Roquefort, blue cheese, pineapple, dates, or nuts.

How to store: Since cream cheese has a relatively high moisture content, it is quite perishable and must be refrigerated. Wrap tightly in moistureproof wrap and use within a few days. Cream cheese may be frozen but will appear slightly dry in texture after thawing.

How to use: The mild, slightly acidic flavor of cream cheese lends itself to a wide variety of uses. Unlike most cheeses, its flavor is more distinct when chilled.

Delicious served alone or with fresh fruit, cream cheese is excellent for use in dips, frostings, spreads, salads, salad dressings, and sauces. Also important in baked products, it is used in cakes, cookies, breads, pies, and refrigerated desserts. Cream cheese is the basic ingredient for the popular cheesecake dessert. When blended with other ingredients, as in making dips or frostings, cream cheese is more easily combined if allowed to soften first at room temperature. (See also *Cheese.*)

Assorted fruits ring-around fluffy Cherry Cream Dressing. Swirl red food coloring in dressing for marbled effect. Accompany with a variety of hot quick breads for a light luncheon.

Cherry-Cream Dressing

    1 3-ounce package cream cheese,
      softened
    2 tablespoons mayonnaise or
      salad dressing
    2 tablespoons maraschino cherry
      juice
    1 tablespoon milk
    2 teaspoons lemon juice
      Few drops red food coloring

         •   •   •

    1 2-ounce package dessert topping
      mix
    1 tablespoon finely chopped
      maraschino cherries

In small mixing bowl combine softened cream cheese, mayonnaise or salad dressing, maraschino cherry juice, milk, lemon juice, and few drops red food coloring. Beat till smooth.

Prepare dessert topping mix according to package directions; fold into cheese mixture. Stir in chopped maraschino cherries. Chill.

To serve, whip chilled dressing till fluffy; pile into serving bowl. Drop one drop red food coloring atop; swirl. Makes about 1⅓ cups.

Cream Cheese Frosting

    1 3-ounce package cream cheese,
      softened
    1 tablespoon butter or margarine,
      softened
    1 teaspoon vanilla
    2 cups sifted confectioners'
      sugar
      Milk
    ½ cup chopped pecans (optional)

In small mixing bowl combine softened cream cheese, butter or margarine, and vanilla. Beat at low speed on electric mixer till light. Gradually add sifted confectioners' sugar, beating till fluffy. If necessary, add milk to make frosting of spreading consistency.

Stir in chopped pecans, if desired. Frosts one 8- or 9-inch square cake.

Chocolate-Cream Cheese Frosting: Prepare Cream Cheese Frosting, *except omit vanilla.* Melt one 1-ounce square unsweetened chocolate; cool. Add to cheese with butter. Continue according to recipe directions above.

Shrimp-Cheese Turnovers

    ½ cup butter or margarine
    1 3-ounce package cream cheese,
      softened
    1 cup sifted all-purpose flour
    1 5-ounce jar process cheese spread
      with pimiento
    1 4½-ounce can shrimp, drained
      and cut up

Cut butter and cream cheese into flour till mixture resembles coarse crumbs. Shape dough into a ball; chill 1 hour.

On lightly floured surface roll dough to ⅛ inch thickness; cut in circles with 2-inch round cutter. Dot rounds with cheese spread and sprinkle with cut-up shrimp pieces. Fold over each round into half circle; seal edges.

Bake on *ungreased* baking sheet at 375° till golden brown, about 15 minutes. Makes 36.

Marble Cheesecake

  2½ cups crushed vanilla wafers
    ½ cup butter or margarine, melted
    ½ cup sugar
    1 envelope (1 tablespoon) unflavored
      gelatin
    1 cup milk
    1 8-ounce package cream cheese,
      softened
    ½ cup sugar
  1½ teaspoons vanilla
    1 14-ounce can evaporated milk,
      chilled icy cold (1⅔ cups)
    ¼ cup unsweetened cocoa powder

Combine vanilla wafer crumbs and melted butter. Press on bottom and sides of 9-inch springform pan or 13x9x2-inch baking pan. Chill.

Combine ½ cup sugar and gelatin in saucepan. Stir in 1 cup milk. Heat and stir till sugar and gelatin dissolve. Cool till mixture begins to thicken. Meanwhile, beat together softened cream cheese, ½ cup sugar, and vanilla; blend in thickened gelatin mixture.

Whip *chilled* evaporated milk to stiff peaks; fold into cheese mixture. Place ⅓ of the mixture in small bowl. Gently fold in cocoa. Alternately spoon vanilla and chocolate mixtures into chilled crust; swirl. Chill 8 hours or overnight. Makes 8 to 10 servings.

Cherry-Cheese Dessert Pizza

> Plain Pastry for 2-crust 9-
> inch pie (See *Pastry*)
>
> • • •
>
> 1 8-ounce package cream cheese,
> softened
> ½ cup sugar
> 2 eggs
> ⅓ cup chopped walnuts
> 1 teaspoon vanilla
>
> • • •
>
> 2 21-ounce cans cherry pie
> filling
> Whipped cream cheese *or* whipped
> cream

On lightly floured surface roll pastry to 14-inch circle; place in 12-inch pizza pan. Flute edges; prick crust. Bake at 350° for 15 minutes. Meanwhile, blend softened cream cheese with sugar; add eggs and beat well. Stir in nuts and vanilla. Pour into partially baked crust and bake 10 minutes longer; cool.

Spread cherry pie filling over cooled cheese layer. Chill. Top chilled pie with dollops of whipped cream cheese *or* whipped cream. To serve, cut in wedges. Makes 10 to 12 servings.

Cream Cheese Cookies

> 1 cup butter or margarine,
> softened
> 2 3-ounce packages cream cheese,
> softened
> 1 cup sugar
> ¼ teaspoon salt
> 1 teaspoon vanilla
> 1 egg
> 2 tablespoons milk
> 2 cups sifted all-purpose flour
> ½ cup flaked coconut, toasted
> Walnut halves (optional)

In mixing bowl cream together softened butter or margarine, softened cream cheese, sugar, salt, and vanilla. Add egg and milk; beat well. Stir in flour and toasted coconut.

Drop cookie dough from teaspoon onto *ungreased* cookie sheet. Top each cookie with walnut half, if desired. Bake at 325° till done, about 20 minutes. Remove cookies to cooling rack. Makes 5 dozen small cookies.

Fruit Cocktail Smoothee

Prepare one 3¾-ounce package strawberry whipped dessert mix following package directions. Drain one 16-ounce can fruit cocktail, reserving ¾ cup syrup. Add reserved syrup to one 8-ounce package cream cheese, softened; beat smooth. Fold in strawberry dessert.

Prepare one 2-ounce package dessert topping mix following package directions; fold into cream cheese mixture. Chill till partially set; fold in fruit. Spoon into sherbet dishes. Chill 5 to 6 hours. Makes 8 to 10 servings.

CREAMED FOOD—Food served in a white sauce made with milk or a combination of milk and cream. Meat, fish, and poultry are often prepared in this manner and served over toast, noodles, or rice. Vegetables may also be served creamed over toast or as a main dish accompaniment.

Creamed Peas and New Potatoes

> 1½ pounds tiny new potatoes
> (about 15)
> 1 to 1½ cups fresh peas (1 to
> 1½ pounds in shell)
> 3 tablespoons sliced green onion
> 4 tablespoons butter or margarine
> 4 teaspoons all-purpose flour
> 1 cup milk

Scrub potatoes; peel off narrow strip around center of each. Cook in boiling, salted water till tender, about 15 to 20 minutes; drain.

Meanwhile, cook peas and onion in small amount of boiling, salted water till tender, about 8 to 15 minutes; drain.

In saucepan melt butter; blend in flour and dash salt. Add milk all at once. Cook quickly, stirring constantly, till mixture thickens and bubbles. Add drained vegetables; heat through. Makes 4 to 6 servings.

A show-off dessert

Convenient canned pie filling tops rich, → creamy cheese layer baked in pastry crust for colorful Cherry-Cheese Dessert Pizza.

These peppermint-flavored, creamy Mint Wafers are made in a jiffy from a frosting mix. Also try different colors and flavors.

CREAM MINT—Small, delicately flavored fondant patties, often softly colored as a key to flavor. Peppermint, lemon, wintergreen, lime, orange, and cinnamon are common flavorings used for these candies. (See also *Fondant.*)

Mint Wafers

        3 tablespoons butter or margarine
        3 tablespoons milk
        1 package creamy white frosting
            mix (for 2-layer cake)
            Several drops oil of peppermint

Melt butter with milk in top of double boiler. Add frosting mix; stir till smooth. Cook over rapidly boiling water for 5 minutes, stirring occasionally. Add flavoring and desired food coloring. Drop from teaspoon onto waxed paper, swirling tops of candies with teaspoon. (Keep candy over hot water while dropping wafers. If mixture thickens, add a few drops hot water.) Cool till firm. Makes 5 dozen.

CREAM OF TARTAR—A powdery white, natural fruit acid (potassium acid tartrate) derived from grapes.

Prior to the introduction of baking powder, cream of tartar was one of the acid ingredients frequently used in combination with baking soda as a leavening agent. Later cream of tartar and baking soda were combined in specific proportions to form baking powder. Cream of tartar is still used as one of the acid ingredients in tartrate baking powder.

The main home uses for cream of tartar are in angel cakes, in candies, and in beating egg whites. Angel cakes containing cream of tartar are whiter and have a finer grain than cakes made without this ingredient. Fondant-type candies are whiter when cream of tartar is added. The addition of small amount of cream of tartar when beating egg whites gives a firmer egg white foam that's more heat stable.

CREAM PIE—A single-crust, cream-filled pie, often topped with a meringue.

The cream filling is thickened with both eggs and starch—cornstarch or flour. Usually, the egg yolks are used in the filling and the egg whites are reserved for the meringue. Milk, water, and fresh or canned fruit juice are the liquid ingredients commonly used in cream fillings.

Since the starch takes longer to thicken than the egg, the starch-liquid part of the filling is cooked briefly before the egg is added. The filling is then cooked a few minutes more to cook the egg.

Cooking cream pie fillings

Cook cream fillings only the specified time. Overcooking causes the starch to break down and lose its thickening power.

Although the basic cream filling is usually vanilla, banana, coconut, or almond flavorings may be added for variety. Other popular variations include butterscotch, chocolate, and lemon cream pies. A fluffy meringue or a thick layer of whipped cream adds the final touch to a cream pie.

Cream pies that are allowed to stand without refrigeration are quite susceptible to food poisoning organisms. Therefore, it is particularly important to store cream pies in the refrigerator promptly. Most cream pies, however, cannot be frozen satisfactorily. (See also *Pie*.)

Banana-Apricot Pie

  2 cups snipped dried apricots
1¼ cups sugar
  3 tablespoons all-purpose flour
  3 beaten egg yolks
  2 tablespoons butter or margarine
  2 medium bananas, sliced (2 cups)
  1 *baked* 9-inch pastry shell,
     cooled
    Meringue

Combine apricots and 1½ cups water. Cover; simmer till tender, about 10 minutes. Combine sugar, flour, and ¼ teaspoon salt; stir into apricot mixture. Cook till boiling; boil 2 minutes, stirring constantly. Stir small amount hot mixture into egg yolks; return to hot mixture. Cook and stir till boiling. Stir in butter.

Place sliced bananas in bottom of pastry shell; top with apricot filling. Spread Meringue over hot filling; seal to edge. Bake at 350° for 12 to 15 minutes. Cool before serving.

Meringue: Beat 3 egg whites with ½ teaspoon vanilla and ¼ teaspoon cream of tartar till soft peaks form. Gradually add 6 tablespoons sugar, beating till stiff and glossy peaks form and all of the sugar is dissolved.

Strawberry-Pineapple Cream Pie

  1 3- *or* 3¼-ounce package *regular*
    vanilla pudding mix
1½ cups milk
  1 8¾-ounce can crushed pineapple,
    well drained (⅔ cup)
  1 teaspoon vanilla
  ½ cup whipping cream
  1 *baked* 9-inch pastry shell,
    cooled
     · · ·
  3 cups fresh strawberries
  ½ cup water
  ¼ cup sugar
  2 teaspoons cornstarch
    Red food coloring

Prepare vanilla pudding mix according to package directions *using the 1½ cups milk.* Cool slightly without stirring. Fold in drained pineapple and vanilla. Whip cream; fold into vanilla pudding mixture. Spread in cooled, baked pastry shell. Chill till set.

In small saucepan crush ½ *cup* of the fresh strawberries; add water. Cook 2 minutes and sieve. Combine sugar and cornstarch; gradually stir in sieved berries. Return mixture to saucepan and cook, stirring constantly, till mixture is thickened and clear. Tint to desired color with red food coloring.

Slice remaining fresh strawberries in half lengthwise, reserving a few perfect whole strawberries for center of pie. Arrange sliced berries over cream filling; spoon strawberry glaze over. Chill several hours. Serve topped with dollop of whipped cream, if desired.

Stir small amount of hot mixture into beaten egg yolks. Slowly add to hot mixture.

Pour hot cream filling into cooled, baked pastry shell; top with fluffy meringue.

To prevent meringue from shrinking, carefully seal to edge of pastry all around.

Lemonade Meringue Pie

A refreshingly different pie—

   1 cup dairy sour cream
   3 slightly beaten egg yolks
   1 4½- or 5-ounce package regular
      vanilla pudding mix
1¼ cups milk
 ⅓ cup frozen lemonade concentrate,
      thawed

     • • •

   1 9-inch *baked* pastry shell,
      cooled
    Meringue

In saucepan combine diary sour cream and egg yolks. Stir in vanilla pudding mix, milk, and lemonade concentrate. Cook, stirring constantly, till mixture thickens and boils. Remove from heat; spoon into cooled pastry shell. Spread Meringue atop hot filling, sealing to edges of pastry. Bake at 350° till golden brown, about 12 to 15 minutes. Cool; chill.

Meringue: Beat 3 egg whites, ½ teaspoon vanilla, and ¼ teaspoon cream of tartar till soft peaks form. Gradually add 6 tablespoons sugar, beating to stiff peaks. Spread on pie.

Chocolate Truffle Pie

   2 cups milk
   2 1-ounce squares unsweetened
      chocolate, broken
   1 cup sugar
 ¼ cup cornstarch
 ¼ teaspoon salt
   2 eggs
1½ teaspoons vanilla

     • • •

   1 9-inch unbaked pastry shell
    Whipped cream

In saucepan heat milk and chocolate over medium-low heat, stirring till blended. In bowl combine sugar, cornstarch, and salt. Beat eggs just till blended; add to sugar mixture along with vanilla. Stir to blend. Gradually stir in chocolate mixture. Pour into pastry shell.

Bake at 400° for 35 minutes, covering crust with foil during last 10 to 15 minutes. Cool. (Filling will thicken somewhat on cooling.) Garnish with dollops of whipped cream.

Orange Meringue Pie

 ¾ cup sugar
 ¼ cup cornstarch
1½ cups orange juice
   2 slightly beaten egg yolks
   1 tablespoon butter or margarine
   1 teaspoon grated orange peel
   1 8-inch *baked* pastry shell,
      cooled

     • • •

   2 egg whites
 ¼ cup sugar

In saucepan combine the ¾ cup sugar, the cornstarch, and ¼ teaspoon salt. Gradually stir in orange juice. Cook and stir over high heat till thickened and bubbly. Reduce heat. Cook 1 minute more; remove from heat. Stir small amount hot mixture into egg yolks; return to hot mixture. Cook and stir over medium heat 2 minutes more. Stir in butter and orange peel. Pour into pastry shell.

Beat egg whites to soft peaks; gradually beat in the ¼ cup sugar till stiff peaks form. Spread meringue over hot filling, sealing to edge of crust. Bake at 400° till golden brown, about 7 to 9 minutes. Let cool on rack before serving.

Spiced Butterscotch Pie

   1 stick piecrust mix
 ¼ cup finely chopped nuts
   1 4-ounce package regular butter-
      scotch pudding mix
 ½ teaspoon ground cinnamon
 ¼ teaspoon ground nutmeg
    Dash ground ginger
 ½ cup whipping cream

Prepare pastry according to package directions. Roll out and sprinkle with nuts; roll lightly to press in. Fit pastry into 8-inch pie plate; flute edge. With a fork, prick bottom and sides. Bake according to package directions; cool.

In saucepan combine butterscotch pudding mix, ground cinnamon, ground nutmeg, and ground ginger. Cook according to package directions. Cool 5 minutes; turn into pastry shell. Cover surface of pudding with waxed paper. Chill. Remove waxed paper from pie. Whip cream; spread atop pie. Sprinkle with additional chopped nuts, if desired.

Mince Cream Pie

1½ cups prepared mincemeat
1 8-inch *baked* pastry shell,
   cooled

. . .

1 3x1½-inch strip orange peel
1½ cups milk
1 3¾- or 3⅝-ounce package
   instant vanilla pudding mix
   Ground nutmeg

Spoon prepared mincemeat into cooled pastry shell. Place orange peel in blender container; cover and turn blender on and off quickly to chop peel. Add milk and *instant* vanilla pudding mix to chopped orange peel in blender container. Cover; blend 5 seconds.

Pour pudding mixture over mincemeat in pastry shell; sprinkle with a little ground nutmeg. Chill thoroughly before serving.

Cherry Cream Pie

In saucepan combine ¾ cup sugar, 3 tablespoons cornstarch, and ¼ teaspoon salt. Gradually stir in 2 cups milk. Cook over medium-high heat, stirring till mixture thickens and bubbles. Cook and stir 1 minute longer. Remove from heat. Stir small amount of hot mixture into 2 slightly beaten eggs. Return to hot mixture; cook 2 minutes longer, stirring constantly. Remove from heat. Stir in 2 tablespoons butter or margarine and 1 teaspoon vanilla. Pour the mixture into one 9-inch *baked* pastry shell. Chill thoroughly.

Stir ¼ teaspoon almond extract into one 21-ounce can cherry pie filling. Spoon over cream filling. Chill pie thoroughly.

CREAM PUFF—Light, hollow puff filled with a sweet, savory filling. In France, cream puff pastry is called *chou* which literally means "cabbage." This name is applied because the finished puff vaguely resembles a miniature cabbage.

Although classed as a pastry, cream puffs are quite different from other types of pastry. They contain a large proportion of fat and eggs and are leavened by steam. The fat is responsible for the tenderness of cream puffs, and the eggs help to form the shell of the puff structure.

The most frequent criticism of cream puffs concerns sunken puffs. When the baked puffs are removed from the oven, they are golden brown and puffy. Their structure, however, is still very delicate and may collapse. This can be prevented by immediately puncturing or splitting each puff and returning it to the still-warm oven to dry out. Even after drying, the puff may have a slightly soggy center. This excess membrane may be removed, if desired, to leave a crisp, hollow puff.

Because their puffs always fall, many homemakers consider cream puffs difficult to make, and avoid doing so. However, once the technique for making them has been mastered, cream puffs become a versatile food that can be used as the basis for appetizers, main dishes, or desserts.

Cream Puffs

½ cup butter or margarine
1 cup sifted all-purpose flour
¼ teaspoon salt
4 eggs

In saucepan melt butter or margarine in 1 cup boiling water. Add flour and salt all at once; stir vigorously. Cook and stir till mixture forms a ball that doesn't separate. Remove from heat; cool slightly. Add eggs, one at a time, beating after each till smooth.

Drop by heaping tablespoons, 3 inches apart, on greased baking sheet. Bake at 450° for 15 minutes, then at 325° for 25 minutes. Remove from oven; split. Turn oven off; put cream puffs back in to dry, about 20 minutes. Cool on rack. Makes 10 cream puffs.

These delight-filled puffs can be tightly covered and stored for a short time in the refrigerator. Unfilled cream puffs can be frozen for longer periods of storage.

By varying the size and filling, cream puffs can be a dainty appetizer, a hearty main dish, or a luscious dessert. Miniature puffs filled with cheese spread, seafood salad, or other savory ingredients start any meal out right. Man-sized puffs overflowing with an à la king or meat salad will satisfy even the heartiest appetite.

For an elegant dessert,
serve Custard-Filled Cream Puffs
topped with rich Chocolate Sauce and
chopped nuts. Use the extra
Chocolate Sauce to make ice cream sundaes.

Cream puffs are most often used as a dessert. A crisp puff filled with a cream filling and topped with a smooth sauce is a big favorite with many people. For a lighter dessert, fill puffs with whipped cream. Cream puffs add a special touch to any meal. (See also *Dessert*.)

Ham and Eggs in Caraway Puffs

¼ cup butter or margarine
½ cup sifted all-purpose flour
2 eggs
2 teaspoons caraway seed
3 tablespoons butter or margarine
3 tablespoons all-purpose flour
2 cups milk
1 cup cubed fully cooked ham
4 hard-cooked eggs, sliced
1 tablespoon chopped canned
    pimiento
¼ cup chopped green pepper

In small saucepan melt the ¼ cup butter or margarine in ½ cup boiling water. Add the ½ cup all-purpose flour and ⅛ teaspoon salt; stir vigorously. Cook and stir till mixture forms a ball that doesn't separate. Remove from heat and cool slightly. Add 2 eggs, one at a time, beating vigorously after each till mixture is smooth. Stir in caraway seed.

Drop dough by heaping tablespoons, 3 inches apart, on greased baking sheet. Bake at 450° for 15 minutes, then at 325° for 25 minutes. Remove cream puffs from the oven; split. Turn oven off and put cream puffs back in oven to dry, about 20 minutes.

Meanwhile, for filling, melt 3 tablespoons butter or margarine in saucepan over low heat. Blend in 3 tablespoons flour, ½ teaspoon salt, and dash pepper. Add milk all at once. Cook quickly, stirring constantly, till mixture thickens and bubbles. Add cubed ham, sliced hard-cooked eggs, chopped pimiento, and chopped green pepper; heat through. Spoon into cream puffs; serve immediately. Serves 4 or 5.

Custard-Filled Cream Puffs

Cream Puffs (see page 691 for
recipe)
⅔ cup sugar
2 tablespoons all-purpose flour
2 tablespoons cornstarch
½ teaspoon salt
3 cups milk
2 slightly beaten egg yolks
2 teaspoons vanilla
1 cup whipping cream
Chocolate Sauce

Prepare cream puffs; bake. Split and return to
oven to dry; cool.

In saucepan combine sugar, flour, cornstarch,
and salt. Gradually stir in milk. Cook and stir
till mixture thickens and boils; cook and stir
2 to 3 minutes longer. Stir a little hot mixture
into slightly beaten egg yolks; return to hot
mixture. Cook and stir till mixture just boils.
Add vanilla; cool. Beat smooth. Whip cream;
fold into cooled mixture.

Fill cream puffs with cooled filling. Top with
Chocolate Sauce. Makes 10 puffs.

Chocolate Sauce: In small saucepan melt
three 1-ounce squares unsweetened chocolate;
cool. In saucepan combine 1 cup sugar, ¾ cup
water, and ½ cup light corn syrup; bring to
boiling. Gradually add hot mixture to melted
chocolate, blending well. Boil gently 10 to 15
minutes, stirring occasionally. Add 1 teaspoon
vanilla. Cover entire surface with clear plastic
wrap; cool. Makes 1⅔ cups sauce.

Chocolate-Pecan Cream Puffs

½ cup butter or margarine
1 cup sifted all-purpose flour
3 tablespoons unsweetened cocoa
powder
1 tablespoon sugar
4 eggs
½ cup chopped pecans
Coffee ice cream
Marshmallow Sauce

Melt butter or margarine in 1 cup boiling water. Sift together flour, ¼ teaspoon salt, cocoa
powder, and sugar. Add to butter-water mixture all at once; stir vigorously. Cook, stirring
constantly, till mixture forms a ball that does
not separate. Remove from heat; cool slightly.
Add eggs, one at a time, beating vigorously
after each till smooth. Stir in pecans.

Drop dough by heaping tablespoons onto
greased baking sheet. Bake at 450° for 10 minutes, then at 325° for 20 minutes. Remove from
oven; split. Turn oven off; return puffs to oven
to dry, about 20 minutes. Remove excess soft
centers. Cool. At serving time, fill with ice cream;
top with Marshmallow Sauce. Makes 10.

Marshmallow Sauce: In 2-quart saucepan
combine 1½ cups sugar, 1 cup light cream, ¼
pound marshmallows (16 to 20), and dash salt.
Cook and stir till mixture is boiling; then cook
over medium heat till candy thermometer
reaches 224°, about 8 to 10 minutes. Remove
from heat; add ¼ cup butter or margarine.
Cool slightly; stir in 1 teaspoon vanilla.

Follow these steps for perfect
cream puffs. Add the butter
to boiling water. Add flour
and salt at the same time.

Cook, stirring vigorously, till
mixture forms a smooth ball.
Remove from heat; vigorously beat in eggs, one at a time.

Drop dough by spoonfuls onto greased baking sheet. Bake.
Split puffs. Turn off oven; return to oven to dry. Cool.

CREAM SAUCE—A thick sauce made with cream or milk, flour, butter or margarine, and seasonings. It has the consistency of a standard, medium white sauce. Cream sauce is served over vegetables, eggs, fish, and poultry. (See also *Sauce*.)

CREAM SODA—A soft drink made with carbonated water. Vanilla and caramel give flavor and a brown color to the drink.

CREAM SOUP—A soup similar to thin white sauce with vegetable juice, vegetable pulp, or broth from meat, fish, or poultry substituted for part or all of the milk.

Cream soups are thickened with cornstarch, rice, or vegetables. The vegetables are cooked until tender, puréed, and blended with the other ingredients. Or, grated, raw vegetables are added to a white sauce and the mixture is heated to boiling. Seasonings are added, such as onion, parsley, herbs, and spices. Garnishes of parsley, grated cheese, toasted bread crumbs, and pimiento are sprinkled on top.

Serve cream soups either hot or cold as an appetizer or as part of the main course with sandwiches. (See also *Soup*.)

Cream of Tomato Soup

Great with grilled sandwiches—

      1 28-ounce can tomatoes
      2 slices onion
      1 bay leaf
      1 teaspoon sugar
      1 teaspoon salt
    ¼ teaspoon pepper
        • • •
      2 tablespoons butter or margarine
      2 tablespoons all-purpose flour
    1½ cups milk

Combine tomatoes, onion, bay leaf, sugar, salt, and pepper in a 2-quart saucepan. Simmer 10 minutes; sieve. Prepare white sauce by melting butter in saucepan over low heat. Blend in flour and add milk all at once. Cook quickly, stirring constantly, till mixture is thickened and bubbly. Remove sauce from heat and slowly add hot tomato mixture, stirring constantly. Serve at once. Makes 6 servings.

Chilled Cream of Chive Soup

      3 tablespoons butter or margarine
      3 tablespoons all-purpose flour
      1 14-ounce can chicken broth
          (1¾ cups)
      1 bay leaf
      2 tablespoons finely snipped
          chives
      1 cup light cream

In saucepan melt butter; blend in flour. Add broth all at once. Add bay leaf and chives. Cook and stir over medium heat till thickened and bubbly. Remove bay leaf. Stir in cream; chill thoroughly. Serve cold. Serves 6.

Cream of Potato Soup

      2 tablespoons butter or margarine
      2 tablespoons all-purpose flour
    ½ teaspoon salt
        Dash white pepper
      3 cups milk
      2 cups diced, cooked potatoes
      1 tablespoon chopped canned
          pimiento

Melt butter in saucepan over low heat. Blend in flour, salt, and white pepper. Add milk all at once. Cook quickly, stirring constantly, till mixture is thickened and bubbly. Add potatoes and pimiento; heat through. Season to taste with salt and white pepper. Makes 6 servings.

Chicken Velvet Soup

      6 tablespoons butter or margarine
    ⅓ cup all-purpose flour
    ½ cup milk
    ½ cup light cream
      3 cups chicken broth
      1 cup finely chopped cooked
          chicken

Melt butter or margarine in saucepan. Blend in flour; add milk, cream, and broth. Cook and stir till mixture thickens and comes to a boil; reduce heat. Stir in chicken and dash pepper. Heat again just to boiling; serve immediately. Garnish with snipped parsley and pimiento, if desired. Serves 4.

Start the meal with an appetizer of cold soup. Place Chilled Cream of Chive Soup in bowls surrounded by cracked ice for an attractive serving idea and to keep the right temperature.

CREAMY—A term indicating a soft, smooth texture. A creamy food resembles cream in appearance, consistency, or flavor.

CREME (*krem, krēm, krăm*)—1. Cream or cream sauce. 2. A French term for whipped cream or butter and custard used in desserts, such as Crème Brûlét. 3. A liqueur.

There are numerous flavors of crème liqueur. Some of the better-known flavors are *crème de menthe* flavored with mint, *crème de cacao* with cocoa and vanilla, *crème de cassis* with black currants, *crème de fraise* with strawberries, and *crème de café* with coffee. These liqueurs are clear and are available colored or colorless.

Crèmes are used as a drink, especially for an after-dinner drink. The liqueur can be served "straight," over cracked ice as a frappé, or in mixed cocktails. Grasshoppers and stingers are examples of cocktails made with *crème de menthe*. Brandy Alexander and angel's dream are made with *crème de cacao* as an ingredient.

Other uses for crèmes are as a dessert topping and as an ingredient in a dessert. Pour a crème over ice cream, sherbet, fruit, or pastry. Choose a flavor that complements the basic dessert. Good examples of this are *crème de menthe* over lemon sherbet or over a chocolate brownie and *crème d' ananas*, a pineapple-flavored crème, over chunks of mixed, chilled fruit.

As an ingredient, the cremes flavor pies, cookies, candies, and desserts. Examples of specialties made with cremes are grasshopper pie and bananas foster. The first combines the flavor of the grasshopper drink with the fluffy texture of chiffon pie. The bananas foster, a delightful specialty made with *creme de bananes*, is flambeed. (See also *Liqueur*.)

Crème de Menthe Balls

  2½ cups finely crushed vanilla
        wafers (about 60)
    1 cup sifted confectioners' sugar
    2 tablespoons unsweetened cocoa
        powder
    1 cup finely chopped walnuts
    ¼ cup light corn syrup
    ¼ cup white crème de menthe
        Granulated sugar

Combine wafer crumbs, confectioners' sugar, cocoa, and walnuts. Stir in corn syrup and crème de menthe. Add a few drops of water, if necessary, to form mixture into 1-inch balls. Roll in granulated sugar. Store in tightly covered container. Makes 42 balls.

Chocolate-Mint Dessert

  ½ cup graham cracker crumbs
    2 tablespoons butter or
        margarine, melted
            • • •
  ½ cup sugar
    1 envelope unflavored gelatin
    2 tablespoons cornstarch
    2 cups milk
    3 slightly beaten egg yolks
            • • •
    3 egg whites
    ¼ cup sugar
  ½ cup whipping cream
  1½ teaspoons crème de menthe
    2 1-ounce squares unsweetened
        chocolate, melted

Blend cracker crumbs and melted butter. Reserve 1 tablespoon; spread remainder in 10x6x 1½-inch baking dish. Combine the ½ cup sugar, gelatin, and cornstarch; add milk. Cook and stir till boiling. Add small amount of hot mixture to egg yolks; return to hot mixture. Cook 1 minute. Cool till partially thickened.

Beat egg whites to soft peaks; gradually add the ¼ cup sugar. Beat to stiff peaks. Fold into custard. Whip cream; fold into custard. Remove 1½ cups mixture; add crème de menthe. Stir chocolate into remaining mixture. Spread half the chocolate mixture over crumbs; cover with mint layer, then remaining chocolate. Top with reserved crumbs. Chill till firm. Serves 6.

Lazy Grasshopper Pie

Make one 3¾-ounce package vanilla whipped dessert mix according to package directions. Stir in 2 tablespoons green crème de menthe and 1 tablespoon white crème de cacao. Chill till mixture mounds slightly. Pile into *baked* 8-inch pastry shell. Chill. Trim with whipped dessert topping and chocolate curls.

CRÈME BRÛLÉE *(krem brü lā')* —A dessert of baked custard topped with caramelized sugar or a caramel sauce. Crème brûlée is a contrast of flavors and textures—rich, creamy custard covered with the brittle, slightly bitter crust of burnt sugar.

Crème Brûlée

    2 slightly beaten eggs
    2 slightly beaten egg yolks
    ¼ cup sugar
    ¼ teaspoon salt
    2 cups light cream, scalded
  ½ teaspoon vanilla
    2 egg whites
        Dash salt
    ¼ cup sugar
    1 cup sugar

Crenshaw melons, weighing from four to nine pounds, have spicy, pink orange meat surrounded by a thin, green and yellow rind.

In top of double boiler, combine whole eggs, egg yolks, ¼ cup sugar, and ¼ teaspoon salt. Slowly stir in cream. Cook, stirring constantly, over *gently boiling* water, till custard coats metal spoon; cook 2 minutes more. Cool at once, placing pan in sink or a bowl of cold water and stirring for a minute or two. Stir in vanilla. Pour custard mixture into shallow 1½-quart dish; chill.

Combine egg whites and salt; beat to soft peaks. Gradually add ¼ cup sugar, beating to stiff peaks. In skillet heat 3 cups water to a gentle simmer. *Do not boil.* Drop meringue in 6 puffs onto water. Cook, uncovered, till set, about 5 minutes; drain on paper toweling. Arrange poached meringues on custard.

In heavy skillet cook and stir the 1 cup sugar over low heat till sugar melts and forms a syrup. Immediately drizzle from tip of spoon over custard and meringue puffs. Serves 6.

CRÈME PATISSERIE *(puh ti′ suhr ē)* — A cream or custard filling used with pastries such as cream puffs.

CRENSHAW — A globe-shaped melon which is a hybrid variety of muskmelon. The crenshaw has a rounded base and a pointed, slightly wrinkled stem end. The smooth rind with no netting and little ribbing has a green color when immature but turns yellow as it ripens. The thick, juicy flesh of the crenshaw has a full, slightly spicy aroma and rich flavor.

Crenshaw melons are available on the market from July to October. Select ripe melons, those with a yellow gold rind, distinct aroma, and softening at the blossom end. Because these melons are very perishable, cover in clear plastic wrap or plastic bags and refrigerate as soon as purchased. Use within two or three days.

Serve slices and halves of crenshaw as desserts or salads, alone or mixed with other fruits. (See also *Melon.*)

Fancy custard for dessert

Drizzling caramelized sugar over the velvety custard and snowy puffs of meringue, puts the finishing touches to Crème Brûlée.

CREOLE COOKERY (*krē' ōl*) — A cuisine developed in Louisiana and the Gulf States by the Creoles. The food has a unique style influenced by the people, the climate, and the geography of this area.

Creoles are the descendants of the French and Spanish settlers in America. "Creative person" is the Latin translation of Creole, and these persons were indeed creative. They took the best of the French cuisine, borrowed the spicy Spanish seasonings, and incorporated the foods familiar to the American Indians in the Gulf area. All of these were then modified by the remarkably patient Negro cooks who brought their basic cooking techniques with them from Africa.

The foods of Creole cookery are highly seasoned as are the foods in most tropical climates. Creole dishes are often very spicy and very hot, yet the seasonings are balanced so that no one flavor asserts itself over any other flavor.

Because Creole cookery developed along the Mississippi River and the Gulf Coast, fish and shellfish predominate in Creole dishes. The people also took advantage of other native foods in their area. Game and vegetables, such as okra and yams, were used extensively. Rice became the basic starch food and tomatoes a common ingredient in sauces. One of the local seasonings, filé, was introduced to the settlers by the Choctaw Indians. Filé is made of powdered young sassafras leaves and is used in seafood dishes and gumbos to impart the texture of okra.

The Creoles, thus, developed an authentic American cuisine, a blend of the best from the Old and New Worlds.

Typical Creole dishes: The main dishes in Creole cuisine have a number of common ingredients. Most are a combination of rice, tomatoes, onions, and garlic with the seafoods, poultry, and game of the Gulf area. Bay leaves, thyme, hot pepper sauce (a mixture of vinegar and red peppers developed in Louisiana), and filé produce the highly seasoned flavors.

The basis for most Creole cookery is the *roux*. This is a cooked mixture of flour and shortening, sometimes cooked until brown. Then liquids are added. This sauce, unlike gravy and white sauce, is made at the beginning rather that at the end of the preparation of a dish.

A dish such as Shrimp Creole illustrates the Creole-style of cooking. It is a highly seasoned combination of tomato sauce, onion, green peppers (sometimes called bell peppers by the Creoles), and the popular seafood in a dish to be served with rice.

Shrimp Creole

½ cup chopped onion
½ cup chopped celery
1 clove garlic, minced
3 tablespoons shortening
• • •
1 16-ounce can tomatoes
1 8-ounce can tomato sauce
1½ teaspoons salt
1 teaspoon sugar
1 tablespoon Worcestershire sauce
½ to 1 teaspoon chili powder
Dash bottled hot pepper sauce
• • •
2 teaspoons cornstarch
1 tablespoon cold water
12 ounces frozen shelled shrimp, thawed
½ cup chopped green pepper
Parsley Rice Ring

In skillet cook onion, celery, and garlic in shortening till tender but not brown. Add tomatoes, tomato sauce, salt, sugar, Worcestershire sauce, chili powder, and pepper sauce. Simmer, uncovered, 45 minutes. Mix cornstarch with cold water; stir into sauce. Cook and stir till mixture is thickened and bubbly. Add shrimp and green pepper. Cover; simmer 5 minutes. Serve with Parsley Rice Ring. Serves 6.

Parsley Rice Ring: Combine 3 cups hot cooked rice with ¼ cup snipped parsley. Pack into an *ungreased* 5½-cup ring mold. Turn out at once on warm platter.

Creole elegance

Simmer tomato sauce in piquant seasonings → as a rich background for shrimp. Serving Shrimp Creole over rice ring makes the meal.

Specific examples of Creole dishes are the famous jambalayas and gumbos. Jambalaya is a rice dish cooked with tomatoes, onions, herbs, and seafood, meat, or poultry. This dish was probably introduced when the Spanish controlled New Orleans since it resembles the Spanish dish, *paella*. It is eaten as a casserole or a stew.

Jambalaya, a tossed salad, and corn bread or French bread make a complete menu for a lunch or a light supper.

Crab Jambalaya

       6 slices bacon
     ½ cup chopped onion
     ½ cup chopped celery
     ¼ cup chopped green pepper
            • • •
       1 28-ounce can tomatoes
     ¼ cup uncooked long-grain rice
       1 teaspoon Worcestershire sauce
     ½ teaspoon salt
       Dash pepper
       1 7½-ounce can crab meat, drained,
          flaked, and cartilage removed

Cook bacon till crisp; drain, reserving 2 tablespoons drippings. Crumble bacon; set aside. Cook onion, celery, and green pepper in reserved drippings till tender. Cut up tomatoes. Add tomatoes and juice, rice, Worcestershire sauce, salt, and pepper to vegetables. Simmer, covered, till rice is tender, about 20 to 25 minutes, stirring occasionally. Add crab; heat through. Spoon into serving bowl; top with reserved bacon. Makes 4 to 6 servings.

Gumbo resembles a thick soup made with a wide assortment of meat or shellfish, tomatoes, and okra. The name comes from this last ingredient because gumbo is derived from the African word for okra.

Filé is commonly used in gumbo as a substitute for the slippery, smooth texture of okra. Care must be taken that the filé is never cooked because it will become stringy. The spice should be stirred in only when cooking is complete.

A variation of the basic type of gumbo is the *gumbo z'herbs*. This dish contains fresh greens and seasonings.

Gumbo Z'Herbs

     ½ pound salt pork, finely chopped
       1 small head cabbage, quartered
       1 bunch spinach, torn
     ½ bunch turnip greens, torn
     ½ bunch mustard greens, torn
            • • •
       1 tablespoon shortening
       1 small onion, minced
       2 cloves garlic, minced
       1 tablespoon flour
       1 tablespoon vinegar
       1 pod red pepper, broken, *or*
          dash cayenne pepper

Cover pork with water; cover pan and simmer about ½ hour. Drain. Place cabbage, spinach, turnip greens, and mustard greens in large kettle and cover with water; cook till greens are tender, about 7 to 10 minutes. Drain and reserve liquid. Put vegetables in blender container and blend until smooth, or mince finely.

In 3-quart saucepan, melt shortening. Add onion and garlic; cook till tender. Blend in flour. Add greens and salt pork. Stir in enough reserved vegetable liquid to make a thick purée (about 3 cups). Add vinegar, ¾ teaspoon salt, and cayenne. Makes 6 servings.

Gumbo, like jambalaya, is eaten as a main course dish requiring little else to make the meal a complete Creole feast.

Jambalaya and gumbo are frequently made with leftovers or odds and ends of food. This illustrates a trait of the Creoles —they do not waste food, but use leftovers to make many delectable dishes.

Creoles are famous for their many fine soups. Their *bouillabaisse* has been appraised as finer than any soup found in France. Turtle soups, thick and thin seafood mixtures, and bisque of shellfish or game are among a few of their specialties.

Creole Clam Bisque

Combine one 10¾-ounce can condensed clam chowder (Manhattan style), one 10½-ounce can condensed chicken gumbo, and 1 can light cream in a saucepan. Cook till heated through. Makes 4 or 5 servings.

Creole cookery, like French cookery, uses sauces extensively. These sauces usually begin with *roux*, then fish or chicken broth, milk, or wine is added for flavor. Meat, fish, and poultry are frequently cooked in a sauce or served with a sauce, such as the following Creole Sauce:

Creole Sauce

¼ cup finely chopped onion
3 tablespoons finely chopped
   green pepper
1 tablespoon butter or margarine

. . .

1 8-ounce can tomato sauce
1 3-ounce can chopped mushrooms,
   drained
¼ cup water
   Dash pepper
   Dash garlic salt

Cook onion and green pepper in butter till tender. Add tomato sauce, mushrooms, water, pepper, and garlic salt. Cover and simmer 15 minutes. Serve with fish. Makes 1½ cups.

French ancestry is reflected in other Creole foods as well as in the sauces. Many of the desserts are basically French. *Brioche*, a soft roll, and *beignet*, a sweet fritter, are typical French foods incorporated into Creole cuisine.

Other desserts are credited to the Creole's own culture. Calas, for instance, are Creole cakes made with rice and yeast, and fried. Many years ago, these cakes were sold by Negro vendors in the streets of the *Vieux Carré*, the French Quarter of New Orleans. People returning from early Sunday church services would stop to hear the vendors' songs and buy these cakes to take home for their breakfast.

Rich chocolate cake and pralines are also typical Creole desserts. The chocolate cakes are made with brown sugar and sometimes strong coffee to produce an especially tempting flavor. Pralines, made of brown or granulated sugar, cream, and pecans, are a traditional Creole favorite which many tourists choose to send home as souvenirs of their visit to New Orleans.

To temper the sweetness of these desserts, Creole coffee with its strong, rich, chicory flavor can be served. The bite of chicory is often softened by making *café au lait* with hot milk or *café brûlot* with citrus peel, spices, and brandy.

CREPE *(krāp)*—A thin, delicate pancake. The crepe batter is made of eggs, butter, flour, and milk and may be either sweetened or unsweetened. The sweet ones with fruit or custard fillings and sauces are used for desserts. Unsweetened crepes are filled with meat, vegetables, or cheese and served as appetizers or main dishes. Crepes, cut in strips or V-shapes, make interesting garnishes for soups. This is an excellent way to use leftover crepes.

The technique of making crepes can be mastered with the proper utensils and practice. Crepes are cooked in a small,

Taste the excellence of delicate crepes and almond cream filling together in Crepes Frangipane, a treat for all to remember.

heavy skillet. There are special pans on the market with flaired sides. However, a standard six-inch skillet can be used.

To cook the pancakes, butter and heat the skillet. Remove from heat, pour in about two tablespoons batter, and quickly tilt pan so the batter covers the bottom. Now, return pan to heat and brown crepe on just one side. Remove from pan and repeat. When ready to serve, fill the crepes, but remember to place the filling on the side which was not browned so the attractive side shows. (See also *Pancake*.)

Avoid last-minute steps

Crepes can be made ahead of time and stacked with a sheet of waxed paper between each. Refrigerate or freeze the crepes until they are needed.

Crepes Frangipane

    ⅓ cup sifted all-purpose flour
    1 tablespoon sugar
    1 egg
    1 egg yolk
    ¾ cup milk
    1 tablespoon butter, melted
    Almond Cream Filling
    2 tablespoons butter, melted
    ½ of 1-ounce square unsweetened
       chocolate, grated
    Confectioners' sugar

Combine first 6 ingredients and dash salt in blender container or mixing bowl. Blend or beat with electric or rotary beater till smooth. Lightly grease a 6-inch skillet; heat till drop of water dances on surface. Lift skillet off heat and pour in 2 tablespoons batter. Quickly tilt from side to side till batter covers bottom evenly. Return skillet to heat and cook till underside is lightly browned, about 1½ minutes. To remove, invert skillet over paper toweling. Repeat.

Spread about 3 tablespoons of Almond Cream Filling on unbrowned side of each crepe; roll up and place folded side down in 13x9x2-inch baking dish. Brush crepes with the 2 tablespoons melted butter and bake at 350° till hot, about 20 to 25 minutes. Sprinkle tops of crepes

with chocolate and sift confectioners' sugar over all. To serve spoon whipped cream over warm crepes. Makes 10 crepes.

Almond Cream Filling

    1 cup sugar
    ¼ cup all-purpose flour
    1 cup milk
    2 eggs
    2 egg yolks
    3 tablespoons butter or margarine
    2 teaspoons vanilla
    ½ teaspoon almond extract
    ½ cup ground toasted almonds

Mix sugar and flour. Add milk; cook and stir till thickened, then continue cooking and stirring 1 or 2 minutes longer. Beat eggs and egg yolks slightly; stir some of hot mixture into eggs and return to hot mixture. Cook and stir just to boiling and remove from heat. Beat smooth. Stir in butter, vanilla, almond extract, and almonds. Cool to room temperature.

Ignite brandy in a long-handled ladle and spoon over Ham-Apricot Crepes just before serving. It's a dramatic show for brunch.

Ham-Apricot Crepes

Make crepes and sauce ahead, then combine with ham at serving time—

>   1 egg
>   1 cup milk
>   1 tablespoon butter or margarine, melted
>   1 cup sifted all-purpose flour
>   10 thin slices boiled ham
>   1 8-ounce can apricot halves
>   ⅔ cup sugar
>   2 tablespoons cornstarch
>   Dash salt
>   1 12-ounce can apricot nectar (1½ cups)
>   2 teaspoons lemon juice
>   2 tablespoons butter or margarine

Beat egg just enough to blend. Add milk, the 1 tablespoon melted butter, and flour; beat till smooth. Lightly grease a 6-inch skillet; heat. Remove from heat and pour 2 tablespoons batter into skillet; quickly tilt pan from side to side till batter covers bottom. Return to heat; brown crepe on one side only. Repeat with remaining batter to make 10 crepes.

Drain apricots, reserving syrup. Place a ham slice on unbrowned side of each crepe; roll up with a ham slice inside. Place in chafing dish or skillet with apricot halves. Pour Apricot Sauce over all; cover and heat through. Keep warm till ready to serve.

Apricot Sauce: Mix sugar, cornstarch, and salt. Blend in reserved apricot syrup. Add nectar. Cook and stir till slightly thickened and clear. Remove from heat; add lemon juice. Stir in the 2 tablespoons butter till melted.

CREPES SUZETTE (*krāp soo zet'*)—An exquisite dessert made of thin pancakes with an orange-flavored sauce or filling. Crepes Suzette is usually flamed with a liqueur or brandy when served.

The crepes can be made ahead; then, just before serving, roll or fold and heat them in the sauce. Or, the orange-flavored sauce can be spread inside the crepes before they are rolled. The heating and flaming of Crepes Suzette is a spectacular scene to enjoy in restaurants or to perform at home for special occasions.

Crepes Suzette

Delicate pancakes with orange filling—

>   ⅔ cup sifted all-purpose flour
>   2 tablespoons sugar
>   ⅛ teaspoon salt
>   2 eggs
>   2 egg yolks
>   1½ cups milk
>   2 tablespoons butter or margarine, melted
>   • • •
>   ½ cup butter or margarine
>   ½ cup sugar
>   2 teaspoons grated orange peel
>   1 teaspoon lemon peel
>   ¼ cup orange juice
>   1 tablespoon lemon juice
>   Confectioners' sugar
>   ¼ cup orange liqueur or brandy

Measure flour, the 2 tablespoons sugar, salt, eggs, egg yolks, milk, and the 2 tablespoons butter into a blender container or mixing bowl. Blend or beat with an electric or rotary beater until smooth.

Lightly grease a heavy 6-inch skillet and heat till a drop of water will dance on the surface. Remove from heat; pour 2 tablespoons batter into skillet. Tilt from side to side till the batter covers bottom evenly. Return skillet to heat and cook till underside is lightly browned, about 1½ minutes. To remove invert skillet over paper toweling. Cook the remaining crepes in the same manner, greasing pan lightly each time. Keep warm till served.

Cream the ½ cup butter and ½ cup sugar; add peels and juices. Spread each crepe with about 1 tablespoon filling mixture. Roll up and sprinkle with confectioners' sugar. Arrange Crepes Suzette in chafing dish. Heat liqueur or brandy in small saucepan, ignite and pour over crepes. Makes 6 servings.

CRESCENT—A bun, roll, or cookie in the shape of a semicircle, tapering to points at each end. Crescent rolls are also referred to as butterhorns and croissants.

Crescents are most often rich in butter and may have a glaze. They are served as desserts, dinner breads, or sweet rolls at brunches. (See also *Croissant.*)

Spread warm crescent rolls with an orange glaze for a party bread to serve at brunch. Round out the menu with grilled ham and sausages, scrambled eggs, chilled fruit, and coffee.

To make crescents, roll dough into a 9-inch circle and cut into 12 wedges. Grasp each wedge at corners of the end opposite point. Begin rolling dough toward point.

While holding corners, flip point over the rolled dough. Place on a greased baking sheet with point down. Move ends of roll into a semicircle for a crescent shape.

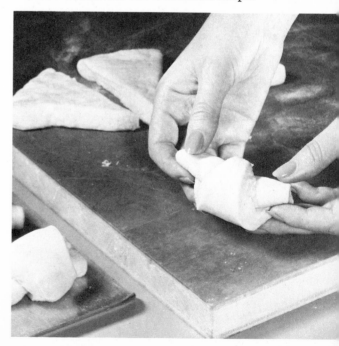

Orange Crescents

> 1 package active dry yeast
> 3 cups sifted all-purpose flour
> 1 cup milk
> ¼ cup sugar
> ¼ cup shortening
> 1 egg
> 1 teaspoon shredded orange peel
> Orange Glaze

In large mixer bowl, combine yeast and *1*¾ cups flour. Heat milk, sugar, shortening, and 1 teaspoon salt just till warm, stirring occasionally to melt shortening. Add to dry mixture in bowl; add egg and peel. Beat at low speed with electric mixer for ½ minute, scraping sides of bowl constantly. Beat 3 minutes at high speed. By hand, stir in remaining flour.

Place in greased bowl; turn to grease surface. Cover; refrigerate 2 hours. Divide in 2 parts. Roll each to 9-inch circle. Cut each in 12 wedges. Starting at wide end, roll up each wedge. Place points down, on greased baking sheets. Let rise in warm place till doubled, about 1¼ hours. Bake at 375° for 10 to 12 minutes. While warm, spread with glaze. Makes 24.

Orange Glaze: Combine 1½ cups sifted confectioners' sugar, ½ teaspoon grated orange peel, and dash salt. Add enough orange juice to make the desired consistency.

CRESS—Plants of the mustard family which have green, glossy, leaves. Some of the varieties are the garden cress or pepper cress, watercress, and Bell Isle cress.

Cress is desirable as a salad green and as a garnish. The pungent flavor accents soup, sandwich filling, and salad while adding color. Seven or eight sprigs of cress add only three calories, yet supply the A, B, and C vitamins.

CRIMP—1. To press food into folds or waves. 2. To gash the flesh of a fish.

Crimping in the first sense is usually associated with making pastry. An unbaked pastry shell is pressed into folds with fingers to make a decorative ridge.

Crimping by gashing the flesh of a fresh or freshly killed fish causes the muscles to contract, which makes the outer layer of the fish crisper when cooked.

CRINKLE—A shaped cookie that has a crackled top. (See also *Cookie*.)

Chocolate Crinkles

Cream ½ cup shortening, 1⅔ cups granulated sugar, and 2 teaspoons vanilla. Beat in 2 eggs, then two 1-ounce squares unsweetened chocolate, melted. Sift together 2 cups sifted all-purpose flour, 2 teaspoons baking powder, and ½ teaspoon salt; add alternately with ⅓ cup milk. Add ½ cup chopped walnuts.

Chill 3 hours. Form in 1-inch balls; roll in confectioners' sugar. Place on greased cookie sheet. Bake at 350° for 15 minutes. Makes 48.

CRISP—A term meaning brittle and firm. Crisping vegetables or crackers restores their firm texture. Vegetables are placed in cold water. Crackers are heated in the oven. Baked desserts with brittle, crumbly toppings are called crisps.

Lemon Crisp

Cream 6 tablespoons butter or margarine and ¾ cup brown sugar. Stir in 1 cup sifted all-purpose flour, ½ teaspoon baking soda, ½ teaspoon salt, ½ cup flaked coconut, and ¾ cup fine saltine cracker crumbs. Press *half* the mixture into an 8x8x2-inch baking pan. Bake at 350° for 10 minutes.

Meanwhile, combine ¾ cup granulated sugar, 2 tablespoons cornstarch, and ¼ teaspoon salt in a saucepan. Gradually stir in 1 cup hot water. Cook and stir till mixture is thickened and bubbly; boil about 2 minutes. Remove from heat. Stir small amount of hot mixture into 2 beaten egg yolks; return to hot mixture in saucepan. Bring to a boil, stirring constantly. Remove from heat. Gradually stir in ½ teaspoon grated lemon peel and ½ cup lemon juice.

Pour sauce over baked crust; top with reserved crumb mixture. Bake at 350° till brown, about 30 minutes. Cut into squares. Serve with whipped cream and twists of lemon. Serves 8.

CRISPER—A drawer or compartment in a refrigerator designed to keep fruits and vegetables at their best quality.

CRISSCROSS—A pattern formed by rows of lines crossing, as in a lattice pie top.

CROAKER—A small, saltwater fish caught in the waters off the Atlantic coast and the Gulf of Mexico. The name comes from the croaking sound made by the fish. The lean-fleshed fish averages about one pound in weight and is marketed whole or as fillets. (See also *Fish*.)

CROISSANT *(krwä sän')*—Rich, flaky, French yeast rolls shaped like crescents. Croissant is the French word for crescent. The flaky texture is produced by rolling and rerolling the fresh dough, layered with chilled butter. Each layer separates slightly as the rolls bake, producing their characteristic light consistency. (See also *Roll*.)

Croissants

1½ cups butter
⅓ cup sifted all-purpose flour

. . .

2 packages active dry yeast
½ cup *warm* water
¾ cup milk, scalded
¼ cup sugar
1 teaspoon salt
1 beaten egg
3¾ to 4 cups sifted all-purpose flour
1 egg yolk
1 tablespoon milk

Cream butter with ⅓ cup flour. Roll mixture between waxed paper to 12x6-inches. Chill 1 hour or longer. Soften yeast in water. Combine milk, sugar, and salt. Cool to lukewarm. Add

Serve buttery-rich Croissants warm from the oven for flaky goodness. Accompany the puffy crescent-shaped rolls with your favorite jams, jellies, and decorative butter curls.

yeast and egg; mix well. Add *3¾ cups* flour or enough to make soft dough. Knead on floured surface. Roll to 14-inch square. Place *chilled* butter on one half; fold over other half; seal edges. Roll to 20x12 inches; seal edges.

Fold in thirds so there are 3 layers. (If butter softens, chill after each rolling.) Roll to 20x12 inches again. Fold and roll twice more; seal edges. Fold in thirds to 12x7 inches. Chill 45 minutes. Cut dough crosswise in fourths. Roll each fourth (keep remainder chilled) to 22x7 inches, paper-thin. Cut in 10 pie-shaped wedges, 4 inches at base and 7 inches long. Put together the extra ½-wedges left at each end.

To shape rolls, begin with base (if dough has shrunk back, pull to original size) and roll loosely toward point. Place 3 inches apart on *ungreased* baking sheet, point down; curve ends. Cover; let double, 30 to 45 minutes. Beat egg yolk with milk; brush on rolls. Bake at 375° for 12 to 15 minutes. Makes 40.

CROOKNECK SQUASH—A kind of summer squash with a curved, swanlike neck. The nubby, warted skin is light yellow in young squash and deep yellow when mature. It grows to be eight to ten inches long and three inches thick. (See also *Squash*.)

Crookneck Curry, served in sauce dishes, combines crookneck squash with a curry mixture to become a vegetable delight.

Crookneck Curry

> 3 medium yellow crookneck
>   squash
> 2 tablespoons butter or margarine,
>   melted
> ¼ to ½ teaspoon curry powder

Cut squash crosswise into ¼-inch slices. Cook in small amount boiling salted water till tender; drain. Combine melted butter or margarine and curry powder with ¼ teaspoon salt and dash pepper. Drizzle over squash. Serves 6.

Confetti Squash

Steam tiny yellow squash (less than 3 inches long) till tender. Split lengthwise and brush with melted butter. Season. Sprinkle with snipped parsley and chopped canned pimiento. Place in shallow pan; heat in 350° oven.

CROQUETTE *(krō ket')* — Shaped balls, cones, or rolls of meat, poultry, or vegetables coated with a savory sauce, crumb coated, and deep fried. They have a crisp brown crust and a tender, moist interior.

Fat-fry small quantities of croquettes at one time to prevent temperature dropping. This assures a crisp, even, brown texture.

Drizzle packaged, frozen peas in cream sauce over crispy ham croquettes. Garnish with green parsley sprigs.

Ham and Rice Croquettes

1 10½-ounce can condensed cream
    of celery soup
1 pound ground cooked ham
    (3 cups)
1 cup cooked rice
1 tablespoon finely chopped onion
1 tablespoon finely chopped green
    pepper
1 to 2 tablespoons prepared
    mustard
1 beaten egg
1 cup fine bread crumbs
2 8-ounce packages frozen peas
    in cream sauce

Blend the first 6 ingredients thoroughly; chill. Shape mixture into croquettes, using about ¼ cup per croquette. Dip in egg, then in crumbs; let stand a few minutes. Fry 2 or 3 at a time in deep hot fat (365°) till brown, 3 to 5 minutes. Check temperature, making sure it remains at 365°. Drain croquettes on paper toweling. Prepare peas in cream sauce according to package directions; spoon sauce over croquettes before serving. Makes 8 to 10 servings.

Ham Croquettes

3 tablespoons butter
¼ cup all-purpose flour
¾ cup milk
2 cups coarsely ground
    cooked ham
1 teaspoon grated onion
    Bread crumbs
2 teaspoons prepared mustard
1 beaten egg
    Creamy Egg Sauce

Melt butter, blend in flour, and add milk all at once. Cook and stir till thick and bubbly; cook and stir 1 minute. Remove from heat. Add ham, onion, and mustard; blend well. Chill.

Shape mixture into 8 to 10 balls. Roll balls in bread crumbs and shape into cones, handling lightly. Combine egg with 2 tablespoons water. Dip into egg and water mixture; roll in crumbs again. Fry in deep hot fat (365°) till heated through, 1½ to 2 minutes. Drain. Serve with Creamy Egg Sauce. Makes 8 to 10 servings.

Creamy Egg Sauce: Melt 2 tablespoons butter; blend in 2 tablespoons flour, ¼ teaspoon salt, and dash white pepper. Add 1 cup milk. Cook and stir till mixture is thick and bubbly. Gently add 1 cup chopped hard-cooked egg.

CROUSTADE *(krōō städ´)*—A term used for a shell or container of toasted bread, shaped rice or pasta, or mashed potatoes. It may be baked or fried, then filled with various creamed meat, seafood, vegetable, or hors d'oeuvres mixtures.

Toast Cups

Trim crusts from 4 slices white bread. Spread bread with ¼ cup softened butter or margarine. Carefully press into *ungreased* medium muffin cups. Toast bread cups at 350° for about 15 minutes. Makes 4 toast cups.

CROUTE *(krōōt)*—Toasted bread cases used for appetizer and dessert fillings.

CROUTON—A small piece of bread, usually diced, that has been oven toasted or browned in a buttered skillet. Croutons are used for garnishing soups, salads, and scrambled eggs; in bread puddings and stuffings; and as casserole toppings.

Serve croutons with bacon bits and shredded Cheddar cheese in small dishes as toppers for hot cooked beans and squash. Save any remaining croutons to add to a green tossed salad. Plan to prepare the croutons and the other toppers a day ahead. Cook six to eight extra slices of bacon at breakfast time. Buy the convenient packaged shredded Cheddar cheese to save preparation time.

Packaged croutons, either plain or seasoned, are available in supermarkets. The seasoned croutons may be flavored with garlic, cheese, or herbs. Heat packaged croutons on a baking sheet in a moderate oven to crisp them before serving.

Garlic Croutons

Vegetables, salads, and main dishes become special courses when topped with toasted garlic cubes—

4 to 5 slices bread
3 tablespoons butter or margarine
½ teaspoon garlic salt

To make croutons, cut 4 to 5 slices of bread into cubes to measure 3 cups. Melt butter or margarine in oven-proof skillet stirring in garlic salt. Drop bread cubes in mixture and toss to coat. Toast in a 225° oven till croutons are quite dry and crispy, about 2 hours. Use as a topper for salads, casseroles, or vegetables, or store in refrigerator and reheat them in the oven on a baking sheet when needed.

Toasted Croutons

Try asparagus, green beans, broccoli, and cauliflower with these crunchy croutons—

Dice white, whole wheat, or rye bread in tiny squares (about ⅛ inch). Brown the bread squares in a little butter in a skillet or the oven, or fry in deep hot fat. Season with salt and pepper, curry powder, or any favorite herb. Serve crispy croutons with cooked vegetables for a zesty flavor and delightful texture or toss atop a big green salad.

Drop diced bread cubes in melted butter or margarine with added seasonings and toss to coat. Heat in oven till dry and crisp.

CROWN ROAST—A roast shaped like a crown and made by sewing rib sections of lamb, pork, or veal in a circle. The ends of the ribs are "Frenched"; that is, a uniform amount of meat (usually one inch) is removed from each rib end.

A crown roast usually will have to be ordered several days in advance. When buying, ask the meatman to tie up the crown, scrape the rib ends, and grind up the scraped meat for the stuffing.

To prepare crown roast, attach aluminum foil to the bone ends to prevent scorching while roasting. Before the end of roasting time, fill the crown center with an herb-seasoned stuffing and roast till done. Unstuffed crown roasts need only be inverted with bones down to form a rack during roasting. Hot vegetables or fruit mixtures can be added to the center of the crown roast before serving.

To carve the roast, insert carving fork firmly between ribs to steady roast and cut downward between the ribs allowing one or two ribs for each slice. Lift slice with knife blade using fork to hold it firm while transferring to plate. (See also *Roast*.)

Ginger-Glazed Crown Roast of Pork

Glossy ginger-glazed crown roast entices company appetites and invites lavish compliments—

  1 4- to 5-pound crown roast of
     pork*

      • • •

½ cup pineapple juice
1 tablespoon minced preserved or
  candied ginger
2 tablespoons light molasses

Place crown roast of pork in shallow roasting pan turning the bone ends down. Insert meat thermometer in loin part of roast, making sure the end of the thermometer does not rest on bone or in fat. Roast at 325° till meat thermometer registers 170°, about 2¼ to 2¾ hours. In small bowl combine pineapple juice, ginger, and light molasses; baste roast with ginger glaze 4 times during the last hour of roasting. Makes 8 to 10 servings.

*Have meatman tie roast securely around loin area as well as near bones. This keeps the tender meat together during roasting.

Turn rib bones down forming a rack if the crown roast is to be filled with potatoes or other hot vegetables after roasting.

Festive crown roast of pork

← Easy-to-carve Crown Roast of Pork filled with tasty stuffing and citrus garnish is pretty enough to set before a king.

Corn-Stuffed Crown Roast of Pork

Set a festive pork crown on the dinner table—

  1 5½- to 6-pound crown roast
     of pork (14 to 16 ribs)
  1 17-ounce can cream-style corn
  1 12-ounce can vacuum-packed
     whole kernel corn, drained
  1 beaten egg
  1 cup soft bread crumbs
  ¼ cup chopped onion
  ¼ cup chopped green pepper
  2 tablespoons chopped canned
     pimiento
  1 teaspoon salt
    Dash pepper

Have crown roast of pork made from strip of pork loin from which backbone has been removed. Have roast tied securely around loin area as well as near bones, and have meat "Frenched" by removing 1 inch meat from rib tips. Season roast. Place in shallow roasting pan, bone ends up; wrap tips in aluminum foil to avoid charring. Insert meat thermometer in loin, making sure it does not rest on bone or in fat. Roast, uncovered, at 325° till thermometer reads 170°, about 2½ to 3 hours.

  To make stuffing, measure and mix remaining ingredients together in a large bowl. An hour before meat is done, fill crown center with Corn Stuffing. Place remaining stuffing in casserole. Dot with butter; bake alongside crown roast at 325°. Garnish with green parsley or citrus fruit. Cut between each roast rib for custom-sized servings. Cut and serve Corn Stuffing along with crown roast of pork.

CRULLER—A twisted or oval-shaped sweet cake made of rolled dough and fat, then deep fried. A sister to the doughnut, the name cruller comes from the Dutch word *krulle,* meaning "twisted cake." Shapes are made by rolling out the dough, cutting it into strips, doubling the strips, and twisting to shape. Braids can be made by twisting two pieces together with ends pinched together. Crullers fried in deep fat swell into golden puffy cakes. Granulated or powdered sugar is sprinkled on the cooked cake as a final step to making sweet crullers. (See also *Doughnut.*)

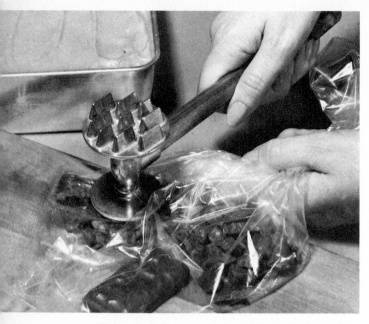

For chocolate-coated candy crumbs, place candies in a plastic bag on a cutting board. Pound with the flat end of a mallet.

Cookie or cracker crumbs are made by crushing the whole cookies with a rolling pin. A blender also makes fine, even crumbs.

CRUMB—1. To coat or bread a food usually with bread, cereal, or cracker crumbs. 2. To crush, roll, or grind a food into fine pieces. 3. A small particle of any food that breaks easily into pieces.

There are numerous ways in which crumbs of one kind or another are used in cooking. Crumbs made from bread or plain crackers may be used to thicken or bind ingredients or to coat foods that are to be baked or fried. Similar crumbs, buttered, top casseroles. Crumbs made from graham crackers, vanilla wafers, gingersnaps, or zwieback make tasty pie shells.

Make your own crumbs, as suggested here, or look for convenience items such as packaged bread, cornflake, and graham cracker crumbs in the supermarket.

Bread Crumbs

Tear slices of fresh bread into quarters. Using small amounts at a time, add to blender. Turn blender on and off quickly till desired fineness results. About 1 slice bread (depending on thickness) makes 1 cup soft bread crumbs.

For fine dry bread crumbs, dry bread in oven. Crush with rolling pin till fine, or break up in large pieces and add to blender container, a small amount at a time. Blend quickly till desired fineness results. Four slices bread (depending on thickness) makes 1 cup crumbs.

Buttery Bread Crumbs

Combine $\frac{1}{2}$ cup fine dry bread crumbs with 2 tablespoons butter or margarine, melted. Sprinkle top of casserole with mixture. Makes enough to trim a 1-quart casserole or four 8-ounce individual baking dishes.

CRUMB CRUST—A crust for an appetizer, entrée, side dish, or dessert recipe made by pressing a buttered crumb mixture into a pan, usually a pie plate. Whether the crumb crust is baked or not depends on the type of mixture used and, often, personal taste. Baking produces a more compact crust that does not shatter easily. (See *Crust, Pastry* for additional information.)

Vanilla Wafer Crust

　1½ cups fine vanilla wafer crumbs
　　　(36 wafers)
　　6 tablespoons butter or margarine,
　　　melted

Mix together crumbs and butter. Press firmly into a 9-inch pie plate. Chill till set.

Graham Cracker Crust

1¼ cups fine graham cracker crumbs
¼ cup sugar
6 tablespoons butter or margarine,
   melted

Combine graham cracker crumbs, sugar, and butter; mix. Press firmly into a 9-inch pie plate. Bake at 375° till edges are browned, about 6 to 8 minutes; cool. If unbaked crust is desired, chill 45 minutes; fill.

To shape an even crumb crust, spoon crumbs in bottom of a 9-inch pie plate. With an 8-inch pie plate, press into crumb mixture.

Loosen a crumb crust by wrapping a hot wet towel around bottom and sides of plate. Hold against plate a few minutes.

Rather moist, compact foods such as blue cheese are most easily crumbled with a fork. Dry foods can be crumbled by hand.

Chocolate-Wafer Crust

Combine 1½ cups fine chocolate-wafer crumbs and 6 tablespoons butter or margarine, melted. Press firmly into 9-inch pie plate. Chill till set.

CRUMBLE—1. A dessert, such as a fruit crisp, topped with a crumbly mixture of flour, shortening, and sugar. The topping bakes to a crisp texture. 2. To break a food into small irregular-sized pieces.

CRUMPET—A soft-textured, unsweetened, English tea or breakfast bread. Once a home-baked delight, now crumpets are produced commercially. The batter, composed of flour, milk, butter, egg, salt, and yeast, is poured into metal rings and baked on a griddle rather than in the oven.

The baked crumpets are split and toasted before being served. Butter and jam are standard accompaniments. Although similar to English muffins, crumpets are softer in texture and are identified by large surface holes that develop during baking. (See also *English Cookery*.)

CRUSH—To apply pressure to food pieces by pounding or grinding so as to break down structure, soften the food, and/or release juices or aroma. For example, fruits are crushed to extract juice for jelly making. Dried bread or crisp cookies are crushed with a rolling pin when a recipe specifies crumbs as a coating or topping for a soft food or mixture. Dried herbs are crushed before using to release flavor.

CRUST—1. The crisp, browned exterior of a baked, sautéed, roasted, or fried food. 2. The baked pastry shell or crumb mixture that lines a pie pan and holds the filling, or the pastry cover for a pie or cobbler. 3. The dough or pastry used to encase small amounts of filling for turnovers or to wrap around large pieces of meat such as baked ham or beef tenderloin. 4. The undesirable drying out of the surface of foods that have not been wrapped or stored properly in the refrigerator or freezer.

When making pies or cobblers, choose a crust from the wide variety available. Besides pastry or biscuit dough crusts, there are chocolate, gingersnap, cereal, coconut, and many others. Some are baked and others are chilled in the refrigerator. The Coconut Crust is an example of a crust which is browned in the oven. The Cornflake Crust will set up when chilled well in the refrigerator. Baking is not necessary.

Coconut Crust

Fill with creamy vanilla or chocolate pudding—

Combine one 3½-ounce can flaked coconut (1⅓ cups) and 2 tablespoons butter or margarine, melted. Press around the bottom and sides of a 9-inch pie plate. Bake at 325° till coconut is light golden brown, about 15 minutes.

Cornflake Crust

Scoop ice cream generously into the shell, then pass a favorite sundae topping—

Combine 1 cup crushed cornflakes *or* crisp rice cereal, with ¼ cup sugar and ⅓ cup butter, melted. Press in 9-inch pie plate. Chill.

Crusts for wrapping meats are generally of two types. In one, the mixture is designed only to hold in the juices during baking. The crust is peeled off and discarded before serving. However, when the dish being prepared is as glamorous as Beef Wellington, the crust, made of puff pastry, is the crowning touch which adds elegance to the final dish. (See *Crumb Crust, Pastry* for additional information.)

CRUSTACEAN—Any of a large class of marine and freshwater animals having crust-like shells. Included are lobsters, shrimp, and crabs. (See also *Shellfish.*)

CRYSTALLIZE—The action by which syrups and jams "sugar" or form crystals as they cool or dry out. Controlling the size and number of crystals is an important factor in successful candy making, particularly when making fudge or fondant varieties. Crystallized ginger and candied orange peel are examples of foods preserved by allowing sugar crystals to coat the outside surface of the food.

CUBA LIBRE—A beverage made of cola and rum, served in a tall glass over ice. It is usually flavored or garnished with fresh lime. (See also *Cocktail.*)

CUBE—To cut solid food into pieces with six equal square sides that are usually larger than one-fourth inch.

CUBE STEAK, MINUTE STEAK—A boneless cut of beef, usually from the round or sirloin tip, which has been tenderized by a machine that breaks up connective tissue in the meat. The machine was originally called a cubing machine; hence, the name of the steak. Today, however, the steak is more frequently marketed as Minute Steak. (See *Beef, Minute Steak* for additional information.)

CUCUMBER—The crisp, green-rinded fruit of a trailing vine belonging to the squash and gourd family. It is also a kin to many melons. Climbing and spreading readily, the stem is stiff and hairy with coil-like tendrils that can be trained to climb. The deep golden flowers measure an inch or

When cubing foods, use a sharp knife to make lengthwise cuts of the desired width. Similar crosswise cuts finish the task.

more across. Although the young fruit is rather prickly, the mature fruit, especially among the hybrid varieties, is smooth.

The cucumber is believed to be native to India, where it has been grown for more than 3,000 years. Early writings indicate the cucumber was served in ancient China and it is mentioned in the Old Testament as a food eaten in Egypt. The Romans devised some hothouse varieties so the fruit could be served daily in the imperial household.

For centuries cucumbers have been served both fresh and pickled. In addition, numerous cosmetic properties have been attributed to the cucumber, and today there are still commercially made skin creams with cucumber as an ingredient.

Nutritional value: Cucumbers are low in calories; thus, they are prized in weight-watching diets. Half a medium cucumber has only seven calories. Because of their high water content, cucumbers are not particularly high in total food value.

Types of cucumbers: Final use, that is whether the "cuke" is to be sliced and served fresh or pickled in a brine, has been the guideline for horticulturists developing the cucumber varieties marketed today. Generally, those suitable for slicing and table use are six to nine inches in length with a dark to very dark green, smooth outer rind. However, for pickling purposes, both commercially and at home, cucumbers from one to three inches in length are the size preferred.

The gherkin, a small cucumber variety native to the West Indies, is always mentioned in a discussion of pickle making. Over the years it has been prized for its use in pickles. However, since small cucumbers of newer hybrid varieties can be mechanically harvested to better advantage, commercial pickle packers depend more upon hybrids than on the gherkin. Homemakers generally make pickles from special pickling cucumber varieties available for planting in the garden.

How to select: Cucumbers, whatever their intended use, should be fresh, firm, bright, and well shaped. Pass up those that look withered or shriveled as they are usually tough, rubbery, and somewhat bitter. Avoid, too, those that have an overgrown, puffy appearance and yellowing rind. Select pickling cucumbers according to the size desired for the type of whole or sliced pickle that is to be made.

How to store: Cucumbers should be washed, dried, and stored in the refrigerator where they will keep satisfactorily for one to two weeks. The edible wax with which cucumbers in the supermarket are sometimes coated to prevent wilting is tasteless. This wax may be scrubbed off or not, depending on your personal preference. However, do not peel cucumbers until just before they are used.

Because of their high water content, cucumbers do not freeze satisfactorily either by themselves or as an ingredient. This is a good thing to keep in mind when making frozen vegetable salads.

Sliced or cooked cucumbers may wilt or become soggy. One to two days in the refrigerator is maximum storage time.

How to prepare: The entire cucumber is edible and certainly looks attractive when sliced crosswise end to end for use on a relish tray or in a refreshing tossed or molded salad. It is no wonder that the phrase "cool as a cucumber" pays compliment to the person who looks fresh and unwilted on a very hot day.

Many people do not think of serving cucumbers as a cooked vegetable. Yet, as members of the squash family, they can be cut up and cooked till tender in boiling salted water. Halved cucumbers with the seeds scooped out may be brushed with butter and baked or stuffed in much the same way as acorn or zucchini squash for a menu change. Butter, salt, and pepper are the simplest of seasoners. A light sprinkle of herbs or a delicate cream sauce goes well with this mild-flavored vegetable, too. (See *Pickle, Salad, Vegetable* for additional information.)

Cucumber tips

• Personal choice or recipe requirements determine whether cucumbers are peeled or not.
• Run tines of fork lengthwise along a cucumber before slicing for frilled edges.
• For crisp slices, put cucumber slices in ice water, or vinegar or sour cream dressing immediately after cutting.

Sour Cream Cucumbers

Thinly slice 1 cucumber; sprinkle with 1 teaspoon salt; let stand 30 minutes. Drain.

Combine ½ cup dairy sour cream, 4 teaspoons vinegar, 1 to 2 drops bottled hot pepper sauce, 2 tablespoons snipped chives, ½ teaspoon dried dillweed, and dash pepper; pour over cucumbers. Chill. Makes 4 or 5 servings.

Salad in a circle

← A built-in garnish of cucumber slices trims this Cucumber Ring Supreme. Cherry tomatoes piled in the center add a bright note.

Vegetable Medley

  2 cups chopped cucumbers
  1 cup sliced radishes
  1 cup sliced green onions
  ½ cup dairy sour cream
  1 tablespoon lemon juice
  ½ teaspoon salt
  ⅛ teaspoon dry mustard

Combine vegetables. Blend sour cream, lemon juice, salt, and dry mustard; toss lightly with vegetable mixture. Chill. Serves 4 to 6.

Cucumber Ring Supreme

    Cucumber-trim Layer
  1 envelope unflavored gelatin
    (1 tablespoon)
  2 tablespoons sugar
  ¾ teaspoon salt
  ⅔ cup water
  2 tablespoons lemon juice
  1 8-ounce package cream cheese,
    cubed and softened

    • • •

    About 6 medium peeled cucumbers
  1 cup mayonnaise or salad dressing
  3 tablespoons finely chopped onion
  ¼ cup snipped parsley

Prepare *Cucumber-trim Layer:* Mix ½ envelope (1½ teaspoons) unflavored gelatin, 1 tablespoon sugar, and ½ teaspoon salt in small saucepan. Add ¾ cup water; heat and stir till gelatin and sugar are dissolved. Stir in 2 tablespoons lemon juice. Pour into 6½-cup ring mold. Chill till partially set. Overlay thin slices from ½ unpeeled cucumber in bottom of mold. Chill till *almost* firm.

Meanwhile, mix the 1 envelope unflavored gelatin, sugar, and salt in small saucepan. Add water; stir mixture over low heat until gelatin and sugar are dissolved. Stir in lemon juice. Gradually beat hot gelatin mixture into softened cream cheese with a rotary beater blending till mixture is smooth.

Halve cucumbers and scrape out seeds; grind using fine blade, or finely shred. Measure 2 cups drained ground cucumber and add with remaining ingredients to cream cheese mixture. Pour over almost firm gelatin in mold. Chill salad in refrigerator till firm. Makes 8 servings.

Ham-Chicken Supreme

6 cups torn lettuce
1 cup diced cucumber
1 medium green pepper,
      cut in narrow strips
1 cup fully-cooked ham,
      cut in strips
1 cup cooked chicken,
      cut in strips
3 hard-cooked eggs, sliced
2 medium tomatoes, cut in wedges
½ cup salad oil
3 tablespoons vinegar
1 tablespoon prepared horseradish
½ teaspoon Worcestershire sauce
2 drops bottled hot pepper sauce
½ teaspoon salt
⅛ teaspoon pepper

Line individual salad bowls with lettuce. Arrange cucumber, green pepper, ham, chicken, eggs, and tomatoes in each. In screw-top jar, combine remaining ingredients for dressing. Cover and shake well. Pass dressing with salads. Makes 8 to 10 servings.

Chilled soups like Buttermilk-Cuke Soup look their "coolest" topped with crisp cucumber slices. (See *Buttermilk* for recipe.)

Cucumber Burgers

Unusual? Yes, but unusually good to eat—

1 medium unpeeled cucumber
½ cup dairy sour cream
¼ cup chopped onion
1 teaspoon salt
1 teaspoon lemon juice
    Dash pepper
1½ pounds ground beef
6 hamburger buns, split

Shred enough unpeeled cucumber to measure ½ cup; drain thoroughly. Stir in sour cream, chopped onion, salt, lemon juice, and pepper. Add ground beef; mix well. Chill. Shape into 6 patties, ¾ inch thick. Broil 3 inches from heat 6 minutes. Turn; broil 4 minutes. Serve in hamburger buns. Makes 6 servings.

Blender Cucumber Salad

How easy it is to let an appliance do all the work for both salad and dressing—

1 large cucumber, peeled
1 3-ounce package lemon-flavored
      gelatin
1¼ cups boiling water
      • • •
1 8-ounce carton cream-style
      cottage cheese
2 tablespoons sugar
4 teaspoons lemon juice
2 tablespoons milk
    Lettuce

Slice cucumber into blender container. Cover and blend on high speed till puréed. Stop blender as needed to push cucumber down from sides. Measure cucumber; add water, if necessary, to make 1 cup.

Dissolve gelatin in boiling water; stir in cucumber. Chill gelatin mixture till partially set, stirring occasionally. Pour into 3½-cup ring mold. Chill till firm.

In blender container combine cottage cheese, sugar, and lemon juice; blend till creamy. Add milk, one tablespoon at a time, till dressing is of the desired consistency.

Unmold salad onto lettuce-lined platter. Pass cottage cheese dressing. Serves 4 to 6.

Cucumber Basket

Hollow out a 3-inch length of unpeeled cucumber, leaving ¼-inch base and walls. Mark lengthwise strips around outside. Cut rind down every other strip of peel, *almost* to base. Crisp in ice water; drain. Cut strips of peel from remaining cucumber. Shape in circles; secure with wooden picks at base of basket. Fill with mayonnaise or salad dressing. Trim with parsley or paprika. Serve with tossed or molded salads. Another time, fill cucumber basket with tartar or seafood-cocktail sauce and pass with fish or shellfish.

Fresh Cucumber Relish

Perky dill-flavored accompaniment to pass with platter of sliced tomatoes or cold meats—

  3 medium cucumbers
  ½ medium onion
       • • •
  ⅓ cup vinegar
  1 tablespoon sugar
  ½ teaspoon salt
  ¼ teaspoon dried dillweed

Slice cucumbers in half lengthwise; scoop out seeds and discard. With food chopper, using coarse blade, grind cucumbers and onion; drain. Stir in remaining ingredients. Chill thoroughly. Makes about 1¾ cups.

Cucumber baskets begin with a hollowed-out chunk of cucumber. Careful marking and cutting of the rind adds decoration.

Cucumber Sauce

So good with fish and seafood—

  1 medium, unpeeled cucumber
  ½ cup dairy sour cream
  ¼ cup mayonnaise
  1 tablespoon snipped parsley
  2 teaspoons grated onion
  2 teaspoons vinegar
  ¼ teaspoon salt
      Dash pepper

Cut cucumber in half lengthwise; scoop out seeds. Shred enough cucumber to make 1 cup; do not drain. Combine sour cream, mayonnaise, parsley, onion, vinegar, salt, and pepper. Blend well. Chill. Makes 1½ cups.

Cabbage-Cucumber Slaw

  3 cups shredded cabbage
  1 cup shredded red cabbage
  1 cup halved slices unpeeled
      cucumber
  ½ cup chopped celery
  2 tablespoons chopped onion
      Salt
      Pepper
       • • •
  2 tablespoons French salad dressing
  2 tablespoons mayonnaise or
      salad dressing

Combine cabbage, cucumber slices, celery, and onion; chill. Season to taste with salt and pepper. At serving time, blend French salad dressing and mayonnaise; toss with cabbage mixture. Makes 8 servings.

CUMBERLAND SAUCE—A thickened sauce of English origin that is served with ham or game meats. Standard flavorings include currant jelly, red wine, orange peel and juice. Flavor is peaked by ginger, dry mustard, cayenne, or lemon juice.

Cumberland Sauce

Combine ½ teaspoon shredded orange peel, ¾ cup orange juice, ½ cup currant jelly, 2 tablespoons claret, and ¼ teaspoon ground ginger in saucepan. Heat till jelly melts, stirring occasionally. Blend 4 teaspoons cornstarch and 1 tablespoon lemon juice till smooth; stir into jelly mixture. Cook and stir till mixture is thick and bubbly; cook 1 to 2 minutes longer. Serve Cumberland Sauce hot or cold with ham or game meats. Makes about 1½ cups.

CUMIN *(kum' uhn)*—An herb related to parsley and a close cousin to caraway. Like some other herbs and spices, cumin has a Mediterranean origin, but its popularity in food has spread throughout the world.

Historical records provide interesting facts on past superstitions concerning the uses of cumin. One of these symbolized cumin as a miser. Another advised a bride and groom to carry cumin during the wedding ceremony to assure themselves a happy life together. Farmers who cursed cumin seed while sowing their crops supposedly were rewarded with a bountiful harvest.

In reality, cumin was used as a drug ingredient in Babylonia and Assyria. Biblical writings list cumin as a tithing spice. In addition, the Greeks and Romans used cumin as a food preservative.

Today, the aromatic seed of the cumin plant, either whole or ground, is the portion used for commercial and home cooking purposes. Although cumin is grown throughout the Mediterranean region, the United States imports are mainly from Iran, Morocco, Lebanon, and Syria.

Cumin's flavor has been described as being strong, warm, and slightly bitter, yet nutty. By itself or as an ingredient in curry powder or chili powder, cumin spices a variety of international foods and beverages, such as Indian curries, hot Mexican dishes, a German liqueur called Kümmel, Arabian salads, and Dutch or Swiss cheeses called Kumminost.

Because of its concentrated flavor, cumin should be added to foods sparingly. It is an excellent appetite stimulant when used in appetizers. It is also recommended for use in soups, sauces, salad dressings, and cookies and with foods such as cheese, egg, cabbage, fish, ground beef, potato, and game. (See also *Herb*.)

Cumin Burgers

Combine 1 pound ground beef, 2 teaspoons instant minced onion, ½ teaspoon salt, ¼ teaspoon ground cumin seed, dash garlic powder, and dash pepper. Shape into 4 patties, ¾ inch thick. Grill over *medium* coals for 6 minutes. Turn and grill 4 to 6 minutes more. Place in 4 buns, split and toasted. Serves 4.

Sour Cream Baked Potatoes

    4 medium baking potatoes
    1 envelope sour cream sauce mix
    ¾ cup milk
    ½ teaspoon ground cumin seed
    2 tablespoons butter or margarine
      Paprika

Scrub potatoes; prick with fork. Bake at 425° for 50 to 60 minutes. Blend together sauce mix, milk, ½ teaspoon salt, cumin, and dash pepper; set aside for 10 minutes. Cut thin slice from top of each potato; discard. Scoop out center of potatoes; add to sour cream mixture. Stir in butter or margarine.

Beat potato mixture till fluffy, adding more milk, if necessary. Spoon mixture back into potato shells. Sprinkle with paprika. Bake at 375° for 20 to 25 minutes. Top with crisp-cooked bacon curls, if desired. Makes 4 servings.

CUP—A small, open vessel with attached handle intended primarily to hold liquids. In the United States, the cup has become a common measuring unit. One standard cup, as determined by the National Bureau of Standards, contains 8 fluid ounces, 16 tablespoons, or ½ pint.

CUPCAKE—A small, individual cake baked in a muffin pan, a paper bake cup supported by a muffin pan, or a small custard cup. Batters for shortened cakes, sponge cakes, and chiffon cakes may be baked as cupcakes. If recipe instructions are not given for cupcakes, use the same baking temperature as recommended for baking the cake in layers, but decrease baking time slightly. If overbaked, the cake texture is dry and top is crusty.

Paper bake cups offer the advantage of serving the cake in the baking cup. If using muffin pans or custard cups, grease well for shortened cake batters. No preliminary treatment is needed, however, with paper bake cups. These are especially good for sponge and chiffon cake batters.

Depending upon the amount of leavening in the cake, paper bake cups or muffin pans are filled about ½ to ⅔ full. If filled too full, the cake overflows the cup as it bakes, forming a crusty rim. If not enough batter is used, the cupcake appears small and sunken when done.

After baking, cupcakes should be cooled on a wire cooling rack before they are frosted. Allow cupcakes baked in muffin pans or custard cups to cool in the pan about five minutes before removing. Using a sharp knife, cut around each cake, loosening the sides from the pan. Invert pan to remove the cupcakes.

Cupcakes may or may not require frosting. Some may be sprinkled with confectioners' sugar or a cinnamon-sugar mixture, while others may have a baked-in topping or filling which takes the place of the frosting. If a frosting is desired, however, the process is quite simple when the cakes are baked in paper bake cups. Dip the top of the cupcake in the frosting and twirl to frost. Cupcakes not baked in paper bake cups may be frosted on sides as well as on top, if desired. This helps to keep the cakes moist. Whole or chopped nuts, flaked coconut, semisweet chocolate pieces, decorative candies, or decorator icing can be used for added trim on the cupcakes.

Cupcakes offer a convenient method for serving cake. They are easily transported, providing an ideal dessert for boxed lunches, picnics, and barbecues. Baked in individual serving portions, they can be pre-pared ahead and stored in the freezer. Shortly before serving time, simply remove the number of cupcakes needed.

Cupcakes are an excellent refreshment for children's parties. Eaten out-of-hand, they are managed easily and cleanup time is minimal. The cakes can be decorated to correspond with the theme of the party. Peppermint candy sticks, animal crackers, decorator alphabet letters, gumdrops, or birthday candles inserted in the top of each cake add special appeal. (See also *Cake*.)

Cranberry Cupcakes

 ½ cup shortening
 1 cup brown sugar
 2 eggs
1½ cups sifted all-purpose flour
 1 teaspoon ground cinnamon
 1 teaspoon ground nutmeg
 ½ teaspoon salt
 ½ teaspoon baking soda
 ½ cup dairy sour cream
 ½ cup canned jellied cranberry sauce
 ½ cup chopped walnuts

• • •

Fluffy Butter Frosting
Canned jellied cranberry sauce

In mixing bowl thoroughly cream together shortening and brown sugar. Add eggs and beat well. Sift together flour, cinnamon, nutmeg, salt, and baking soda. Add to creamed mixture alternately with sour cream and ½ cup cranberry sauce; beat smooth. Add nuts.

Fill paper bake cups in muffin pans half full. Bake at 350° for 20 to 25 minutes. Cool. Frost with Fluffy Butter Frosting. Using hors d'oeuvre cutters, make cutouts from additional canned jellied cranberry sauce. Just before serving, top each cake with a cranberry cutout. Makes about 2 dozen cupcakes.

Fluffy Butter Frosting: In mixing bowl combine ½ cup butter or margarine, softened; 1 egg yolk; 2 tablespoons buttermilk *or* milk; ½ teaspoon vanilla; and 3 cups sifted confectioners' sugar. Blend together. Beat at medium speed on electric mixer for 3 minutes.

If frosting is soft, beat in additional sifted confectioners' sugar to make of spreading consistency. Frosts 24 cupcakes.

Cheese-Filled Chocolate Cupcakes

1 package 2-layer-size chocolate
   cake mix
1 8-ounce package cream cheese,
   softened
⅓ cup sugar
1 egg
1 6-ounce package semisweet
   chocolate pieces (1 cup)

Mix cake according to package directions. Fill paper bake cups in muffin pans two-thirds full. Cream the cheese with the sugar; beat in egg and dash salt. Stir in chocolate pieces.

Drop one rounded teaspoon cheese mixture into each cupcake. Bake according to package directions for cupcakes. Makes 30 cupcakes.

Peanut Butter Cupcakes

Cream ½ cup chunk-style peanut butter and ⅓ cup shortening. Gradually add 1½ cups brown sugar, beating till light. Add 1 teaspoon vanilla and 2 eggs, one at a time, beating till fluffy. Sift together 2 cups sifted all-purpose flour, 2 teaspoons baking powder, and ½ teaspoon salt; add alternately with 1 cup milk, beating after each addition.

Fill paper bake cups in muffin pans half full. Bake at 375° for 15 to 20 minutes. Cool; frost with peanut butter. Makes 24 cupcakes.

Everyday Cupcakes

½ cup shortening
1¾ cups sifted all-purpose flour
1 cup sugar
2½ teaspoons baking powder
½ teaspoon salt
1 egg
¾ cup milk
1 teaspoon vanilla

Place shortening in mixing bowl. Sift in dry ingredients. Add egg and *half* the milk; mix till flour is moistened. Beat 2 minutes at low speed on electric mixer. Add remaining milk and vanilla; beat 1 minute longer. Fill paper bake cups in muffin pans half full. Bake at 375° till done, about 20 minutes. Cool; frost with desired frosting. Makes 18 cupcakes.

Frost cupcakes in a hurry. Dip top of each cake into fluffy-type frosting. Twirl cupcake slightly, then turn right side up.

CURD—The semisolid mass which results from the coagulation of milk protein. A curd is formed when milk sours or when an acid or enzyme is added. The curd, used in cheese, separates from the whey.

CURDLE—To cause the formation of a curd. The curdling of milk is the first step in the making of cheese. In cooking, curdling is undesirable and occurs when milk or sour cream is heated to too high a temperature. Curdling occurs frequently when acid foods are combined with milk, as in the preparation of tomato soup. To prevent curdling, slowly add the acid food to the milk, stirring constantly.

CURED—To preserve food by one of many special processes. Meat and fish may be cured by soaking them in a brine solution, or by salting, drying, or smoking. Cheese is often cured by injecting or spraying with a mold culture. Curing imparts a characteristic flavor and texture to a food, depending upon the curing ingredients and whether the cure is light or heavy.

Festive cupcakes

Fresh-baked Cranberry Cupcakes sport cran- →
berry cutouts nestled in fluffy frosting. Cranberry also is used in the spicy batter.

Curly endive adds variety to tossed salads. Slightly bitter, the tightly curled leaves vary from rich green to yellowish white.

CURLY ENDIVE—A leafy, green vegetable which grows in a bunchy head and is eaten as a salad green. A heavy rib supports the narrow, ragged-edged leaves which are tightly curled. The outer leaves appear darker green, while the inside leaves are bleached. Although higher in vitamins, the darker leaves have a more bitter flavor than the lighter ones. (See also *Endive.*)

CURRANT—1. A small, seedless, raisinlike fruit made from a specific variety of grape which has been dried. 2. A small, round, red berry which grows on a bush of the same name. Although these two fruits carry the same name, they are not related.

Dried grape currants: They were first commercially important in Greece in the sixteenth century. A popular ingredient in cooking, they were exported to France and other European countries. The French called the fruit *raisins de Corinthe* since most of them were imported from Corinth, Greece. The name was eventually shortened and they became known as currants.

Today, the Mediterranean countries are still the major producers of dried currants. However, some are produced also in the United States. They are made from the Black Corinth grape grown in California. In addition to dried black currants, another variety known as white Zante (named after the Greek island which exports them) is available on the market.

Dried currants are quite high in carbohydrates; one-half cup of the fruit provides 208 calories. They also contain calcium, phosphorus, and iron.

This raisinlike fruit has a relatively long storage life and is most often found in the supermarket packaged in boxes. Refrigeration of this fruit is required only after the box has been opened at which time it should be stored in a tightly covered container to maintain freshness.

Used alone or in combination with raisins and/or other fruits, dried currants are usually added to cakes, cookies, and breads. They are more tart and have a more concentrated flavor than do raisins.

Fresh berry currants: The first written reference to the fresh or red berries known as currants dates back to the fifteenth century where they were mentioned as a garden-fruit plant. These berries were probably called currants because they resembled the dried fruit of the same name.

Cultivated best in cool climates, they were first grown in northern Europe. They accompanied the early settlers to America and although they are still produced in the colder regions of the United States, their cultivation is restricted. This restriction is a conservation measure since the currant bush is a carrier of a fungus which destroys the white pine. However, some disease-resistant varieties of currants have been developed, making their cultivation more acceptable. In addition to the cultivated crop, a few wild currant bushes are often found throughout the country.

Fresh currants, much lower in calories than dried currants, contain about 34 calories per half cup. They also contribute vitamin C, phosphorus, and iron.

Three different varieties of fresh currants are grown—red, white, and black. The peak growing season for fresh currants is from June through August. At other times the fruit is available only in the local markets. In selecting fresh currants, look for firm, ripe berries with a good color and attached stems. If purchased for jellymaking, avoid overripe fruit as it does not jell as well as fruit which is slightly underripe.

Fresh currants should be sorted after purchasing and stored in the refrigerator in a covered container. Avoid keeping berries over one or two days as they may soften and become overripe. When ready to use, wash fruit and remove stems.

Fresh currants may be served alone although they usually require sugar as they are quite tart—much more so than dried currants. White currants, the least tart variety, can be served fresh in salads. The most popular use of the red and black varieties is in jellymaking. A famous French jam, *bar-le-duc*, is made by suspending the whole berries in a clear jelly. *Bar-le-duc* is available in specialty shops. Black currants are used also in the making of *cassis*, an alcoholic beverage. (See also *Fruit*.)

Currant-Raisin Sauce

⅓ cup raisins
½ cup water
⅓ cup currant jelly
½ teaspoon grated orange peel
½ cup orange juice
2 tablespoons brown sugar
1 tablespoon cornstarch
Dash ground allspice
Dash salt

Combine raisins, water, jelly, orange peel, and orange juice in saucepan; bring to boiling. Combine brown sugar, cornstarch, allspice, and salt; stir into orange mixture. Cook, stirring constantly, till thickened and clear. Serve warm sauce over cooked ham slice.

Currant Glaze

In saucepan melt ½ cup currant jelly, stirring till jelly is smooth. Add 1 tablespoon vinegar, ½ teaspoon dry mustard, ¼ teaspoon ground cinnamon, and dash ground cloves; blend together thoroughly. Brush ham with fruit glaze occasionally during last 30 minutes of heating time and just before serving.

A traditional dessert for the festive holidays is steamed Black Currant Pudding. Currants, raisins, mixed candied fruits, and almonds add a seasonal note to this moist and delicately spiced dessert. Serve warm with light and fluffy hard sauce.

Black Currant Pudding

A holiday dessert that can be made ahead—

> ½ pound beef suet, ground
> (2¾ cups)
> 2 cups fine dry bread crumbs
> 1 cup sifted all-purpose flour
> 1 cup sugar
> 1 cup finely chopped blanched
> almonds
> 1 cup dried currants
> ⅔ cup mixed candied fruits and
> peels
> ⅔ cup golden raisins
> ½ cup dark raisins
> ½ teaspoon ground nutmeg
> ½ teaspoon ground cinnamon
> ½ teaspoon ground allspice
> ½ teaspoon salt
> • • •
> ¾ cup milk
> 4 slightly beaten eggs
> ½ cup brandy *or* rum
> 1½ teaspoons grated lemon peel
> ¼ cup lemon juice
> • • •
> Hard Sauce

In large bowl combine suet, crumbs, flour, sugar, chopped almonds, currants, mixed fruits, raisins, nutmeg, cinnamon, allspice, and salt; mix well. In second bowl combine milk, eggs, brandy *or* rum, lemon peel, and lemon juice; stir into fruit mixture. Mix thoroughly.

Turn into well-greased 7½-cup ovenproof bowl or mold; cover tightly. Place on rack in deep kettle or Dutch oven. Pour boiling water in kettle to 1-inch depth; cover kettle. Gently boil water, steaming pudding for 5 hours. (Add more boiling water, if necessary.)

When finished cooking, remove mold from kettle. Cool about 30 minutes in mold. Unmold pudding; let stand until completely cooled. Wrap in foil; refrigerate till ready to use.

To reheat pudding, place foil-wrapped pudding on rack in deep kettle or Dutch oven. Use same steaming method given above; steam pudding for 1 to 1½ hours.

Serve pudding warm with *Hard Sauce:* In mixing bowl thoroughly cream together 1 cup butter or margarine, softened, and 4 cups sifted confectioners' sugar. Add 2 teaspoons vanilla; mix well. Makes 12 to 16 servings.

Currant-Orange Chicken

Tart and peppy fruit sauce adds elegance—

> ½ cup currant jelly
> ¼ cup frozen orange juice
> concentrate, thawed
> 2 teaspoons cornstarch
> 1 teaspoon dry mustard
> Dash bottled hot pepper sauce
> • • •
> ½ cup all-purpose flour
> 1 teaspoon salt
> 1 2½- to 3-pound ready-to-cook
> broiler-fryer chicken, cut up
> Shortening
> • • •
> 1 cup chopped celery
> ¼ cup chopped onion
> ¼ cup butter or margarine
> 2 tablespoons frozen orange juice
> concentrate, thawed
> ½ teaspoon salt
> 1⅓ cups uncooked packaged
> precooked rice

In saucepan combine jelly, ¼ cup orange juice concentrate, and ⅓ cup water; cook and stir till jelly melts and mixture is smooth.

Blend cornstarch, dry mustard, and bottled hot pepper sauce with 1 tablespoon cold water; stir into jelly mixture. Cook, stirring constantly, till thickened and clear; set aside.

Combine flour and 1 teaspoon salt in paper bag. Add 2 or 3 pieces of chicken at a time; shake to coat. In skillet brown chicken in hot shortening over medium heat, turning occasionally. Drain off excess fat. Pour currant-orange sauce over chicken in skillet. Cover; simmer over very low heat till tender, about 45 minutes; baste occasionally with sauce.

Serve chicken with Orange Rice: Cook celery and onion in butter or margarine till tender but not brown. Stir in 2 tablespoons orange juice concentrate, 1¼ cups water, and ½ teaspoon salt; bring to boiling. Add uncooked rice; continue cooking according to directions on rice package. Makes 4 servings.

CURRY—Food cooked in a liquid seasoned with curry powder or served in a sauce seasoned with curry powder. Meat, fish, poultry, eggs, vegetables, and fruits may

Curried Ham Rolls add glamour and an intriguing blend of flavors to a late-evening supper. Rice mix adds convenience to this main dish; prepare ahead, then heat just before serving.

be curried. Most readily identified with the cooking of India and countries of the Far East, curry varies from country to country, both in method of preparation and in manner and customs of serving.

A main dish curry is served with steamed rice and assorted accompaniments. A limited number of accompaniments, usually only fresh, grated coconut and a hot mango chutney, are served with an authentic Indian curry. The Americanized version offers additional accompaniments such as nuts, green onions, raisins, kumquats, and peppers. They are served in bowls and sprinkled atop the curry in layers. (See also *Indian Cookery*.)

CURRY POWDER—A ground blend of spices used as a seasoning to impart the characteristic flavor of Indian curry cookery. Sometimes, 16 or more spices are used in making curry powder. Depending upon the manufacturer, each blend differs slightly; however, cumin, coriander, fenugreek, turmeric, and red pepper are found in varying amounts in every curry powder. Additional spices sometimes used include caraway seed, cinnamon, allspice, cardamom, cloves, fennel, ginger, yellow mustard, mace, and black or white pepper.

Curry powder is one of the world's oldest seasonings. Popular in India and the Far East, curry has been used as a seasoning for almost fifteen hundred years. However, Indian curries are most frequently made with a spice blend which is ground daily in the home. Thus, each blend varies somewhat, depending upon how it is used.

The "hotness" of the curry blend differs within the Indian culture. A milder spicing is preferred in the North while in Southern India, the hotter the spice, the better. Red peppers, which are primarily responsible for the hotness of curry, were unknown in ancient curries. These pungent peppers, which originated in the Western Hemisphere, did not become a part of the spice blend until after the discovery of America. Today, red peppers are considered an essential ingredient in all curries.

The popularity of using a highly spiced curry powder in India and in tropical countries is based in part on the effect it has on the body temperature. Eating "hot" dishes promotes perspiration, which in turn, helps keep the body cool. Also, most spices needed for a good curry blend are readily available in tropical climates.

Although the Indian housewife usually makes her own curry blend, commercial curry powders are sold in the bazaars. In the United States mild-flavored commercial blends are used almost exclusively.

As with all spices, curry powder is more flavorful and aromatic when fresh. Avoid long storage and always store in a tightly covered container in a cool, dry place.

Curry powder adds flavor to meats, fish, poultry, vegetables, salads, salad dressings, sauces, and soups. Used sparingly, it enhances the natural flavor of food. For an Indian-type curried dish in which the spice blend dominates the food, a larger amount of seasoning is needed. (See *Spice, Indian Cookery* for additional information.)

Curry cooking tips

A more flavorful curry dish results if the curry powder is moistened or cooked in a little fat before using. Long, slow cooking generally improves the flavor also.

Enhance curry flavor in sauce or salad dressing by chilling mixture several hours.

Curried Ham Rolls

As pictured on preceding page—

      1 6-ounce package curried rice
         mix
    ¾ cup golden raisins
      2 hard-cooked eggs, chopped
      1 tablespoon snipped parsley
      3 tablespoons butter or margarine
      2 tablespoons cornstarch
      1 teaspoon curry powder
    ¼ teaspoon salt
    2¼ cups milk
    12 square slices boiled ham

Cook rice mix according to package directions. Add raisins, chopped eggs, and parsley; mix well. In saucepan melt butter; blend in cornstarch, curry powder, and salt. Add milk; cook and stir till thick and bubbly. Add *half* of the curry sauce to rice mixture; mix well. Place rice in 10x6x1¾-inch baking dish.

With spatula make 5 crosswise indentations in rice starting about 1½ inches from ends of casserole. Put 2 ham slices together; curve to form roll. Insert one side of roll into end of casserole; tuck second side into first indentation. Repeat with 2 more ham slices, tucking first side of roll into same indentation with previously made roll and second side into next indentation. Continue forming rolls with remaining ham. Pour remaining sauce atop. Bake at 350° for 30 to 35 minutes. Serves 6.

Curried Beef Cubes

Cut 2 pounds beef chuck in ¾-inch cubes. Coat beef cubes with ⅓ cup all-purpose flour. In skillet brown meat in ⅓ cup hot shortening. Add 1 large onion, sliced; cook just till onion is tender but not brown.

Combine two 8-ounce cans tomato sauce; 1½ cups water; 1 clove garlic, minced; 1 teaspoon salt; and ¼ teaspoon pepper. Pour mixture over meat. Cover and cook slowly over low heat till meat is tender, about 1½ hours. Stir in 2 to 3 teaspoons curry powder.

Add one 9-ounce package frozen cut green beans to meat mixture. Cook till tender, about 15 minutes, separating beans with a fork as they heat. Serve meat mixture over hot cooked rice or noodles. Makes 6 to 8 servings.

Chicken Curry

Another time serve curry in rice ring—

- 1 tablespoon butter or margarine
- 1 cup finely chopped peeled apple
- 1 cup sliced celery
- ½ cup chopped onion
- 1 clove garlic, minced
- 2 tablespoons cornstarch
- 2 to 3 teaspoons curry powder
- ¾ teaspoon salt
- ¾ cup cold chicken broth
- 2 cups milk
- 2 cups diced cooked chicken
- 1 3-ounce can sliced mushrooms, drained (½ cup)
  Hot cooked rice
  Curry accompaniments

In saucepan melt butter; add apple, celery, onion, and garlic. Cook till onion is tender. Combine cornstarch, curry, salt, and cold chicken broth. Stir into onion mixture; add milk. Cook and stir till thick and bubbly. Stir in chicken and mushrooms. Heat through.

Serve over hot cooked rice; pass curry accompaniments—raisins, shredded coconut, chopped peanuts, and chutney. Serves 5 or 6.

Curried Lamb

- 2 pounds lean lamb, cut in 1-inch cubes
- 3 tablespoons all-purpose flour
- 2 tablespoons butter or margarine
- 1 cup chopped onion
- 1 clove garlic, minced
- 1 to 1½ tablespoons curry powder
- 1½ teaspoons salt
- 1 teaspoon grated fresh gingerroot *or* ½ teaspoon ground ginger
- 2 tomatoes, peeled and chopped
- ¼ cup water
  Hot cooked rice
  Grated raw carrot
  Curry accompaniments

Coat lamb with flour. Brown meat in butter; remove from skillet. Add onion and garlic to skillet; cook till tender. Return meat to skillet. Stir in curry powder, salt, gingerroot, tomatoes, and water. Cover; simmer, stirring occasionally, till lamb is tender, 45 to 60 minutes. Toss rice with grated carrot; serve with lamb. Pass accompaniments—whole preserved kumquats, mango chutney, sliced green onions, golden raisins, shredded coconut, and shelled peanuts. Makes 6 to 8 servings.

Exotic and colorful Chicken Curry offers a new idea for a dinner party. Serve over rice and pass assorted accompaniments—raisins, shredded coconut, peanuts, and chutney.

Curry Salad

For best flavor, prepare dressing ahead and chill several hours or overnight—

    ½ teaspoon beef-flavored gravy
        base
    ¼ cup hot water
    1 cup mayonnaise or salad
        dressing
    1 clove garlic, minced
    1 tablespoon curry powder
    ¼ teaspoon Worcestershire sauce
    6 to 8 drops bottled hot pepper
        sauce

                •   •   •

    6 cups torn mixed salad greens
    4 cups torn fresh spinach
    1 16-ounce can artichoke hearts,
        chilled, drained, and halved
    ¼ cup sliced radishes

To make dressing, dissolve beef-flavored gravy base in hot water; blend into mayonnaise or salad dressing. Stir in garlic, curry powder, Worcestershire sauce, and bottled hot pepper sauce; mix well. Chill thoroughly.

In large bowl combine torn mixed salad greens, torn fresh spinach, halved artichoke hearts, and sliced radishes. Just before serving, toss lettuce mixture lightly with chilled salad dressing. Makes 10 servings.

CUSK—An edible saltwater fish belonging to the cod family. Found in North Atlantic waters from Greenland south to Cape Cod, cusk is characterized by a long black fin extending from just behind the head to the tail. A medium-sized fish, cusks average from 5 to 10 pounds in weight and from 1½ to 2½ feet in length.

Although cusk is most often marketed in fillets, it is sometimes available salted and smoked. Fresh cusk is prepared in the same way as cod or haddock.

Far-East flavor

For a touch of India, serve zesty Curry Salad featuring artichoke hearts, fresh spinach, sliced radishes, and mixed salad greens.

CUSTARD—An egg and milk mixture in which the egg acts as a thickening agent during cooking. If sweetened and flavored, the mixture is served as a dessert. If unsweetened, it is used as a main dish with meat, cheese, or vegetables added.

A dessert-type custard, known as soft or stirred custard, is cooked and stirred over low heat in a heavy saucepan or in the top of a double boiler over hot water. Stirred custard has much the same consistency as heavy cream. If baked in the oven without stirring, it is known as baked custard. The finished product holds its shape when unmolded. Main-dish custards made in a pastry shell generally are baked in the oven and can be cut for serving.

Usual proportions for dessert-type custards are one or one and one-half eggs plus two tablespoons sugar for each cup of milk. For a firmer custard, use more eggs. Likewise, increase the amount of sugar for a sweeter product. Custard is sometimes unmolded and used to make fancy cutouts for garnishing. This type of custard must be quite firm; thus, a greater number of eggs are needed.

Custard substitutions

Basic substitutions are possible in a standard custard which result in a product of about the same consistency. However, the color and flavor may vary slightly.

If several eggs are used, use one of the following substitutions for *one of the eggs:*

    two egg yolks
    two egg whites
    one tablespoon all-purpose flour

Custard is an excellent way of adding to the diet important nutrients which are found in milk and eggs. Due to its soft texture, often it is included in special diets.

Custard should always be refrigerated after baking if it is to be held for any length of time before serving.

To make custard add sugar and salt to slightly beaten eggs and stir in scalded milk, which has been cooled.

For soft custard, cook and stir over low heat in a heavy saucepan or in the top of a double boiler over simmering, but not boiling water. When done, the mixture coats a metal spoon. Immediately remove from heat and place pan in cold water. When slightly cooled, stir in the flavoring.

Custards lend themselves to many variations. Soft custard may be served warm or chilled as a sauce over fruit, cake, or pudding. Popular in England, soft custard accompanies many desserts just as cream often tops off American desserts. Floating island dessert is made by spooning soft meringue atop soft custard.

For baked custard, pour the mixture into individual custard cups or into one large baking dish. Place the cups or baking dish in a shallow baking pan on the oven rack. Add hot water to the baking pan to a depth of one inch and bake at a moderate oven temperature. The custard is done when a knife inserted halfway between the center and outside edge of the custard comes out clean. After cooking, remove from the hot water to stop the cooking.

Baked custard, delicious either warm or chilled, is commonly served with a dash of ground nutmeg or a dollop of tart, red jelly. Variations include the addition of instant coffee powder, unsweetened cocoa powder, shredded coconut, or caramelized sugar. Baked in a pie shell, custard is a holiday favorite when pumpkin is added.

Overcooking custard results in an undesirable product. For a stirred custard, the mixture takes on a curdled appearance due to over-coagulation of egg protein. Although this change cannot be reversed, the appearance is improved somewhat by beating the mixture with a rotary beater. When a baked custard is overcooked, tiny bubbles appear around the edge of the dish, and there is a separation of liquid from solid when the custard is cut.

Main-dish custards, which are unsweetened, add variety to the menu. A custard mixture poured over layers of bread and cheese and baked in a baking dish is known as a strata; in addition, meat is sometimes added. A favorite French dish, Quiche Lorraine, is made with crisp-cooked crumbled bacon and cheese in a custard mixture, baked in a pastry shell.

Toasted Coconut Pie

        3 beaten eggs
   1½ cups sugar
    ½ cup butter or margarine, melted
        4 teaspoons lemon juice
        1 teaspoon vanilla
        1 3½-ounce can flaked coconut
            (1⅓ cups)
            Plain Pastry for 1-crust 9-inch
            pie (See *Pastry*)

            •   •   •

            Whipped cream
            Toasted coconut

Thoroughly combine eggs, sugar, butter, lemon juice, and vanilla; stir in flaked coconut.

Line 9-inch pie plate with pastry. Pour coconut-custard filling into pastry-lined pie plate. Bake at 350° till knife inserted halfway between center and edge comes out clean, about 40 to 45 minutes. Cool. Garnish with whipped cream and toasted coconut.

Caramel Custard Pie

        1 14½-ounce can evaporated
            milk (1⅔ cups)
        2 eggs
        1 cup brown sugar
        3 tablespoons all-purpose flour
        2 tablespoons butter or margarine
            Plain Pastry for 1-crust 9-inch
            pie (See *Pastry*)

Combine evaporated milk, eggs, and ⅓ cup water; beat till well mixed. Set aside. Combine brown sugar and flour; cut in butter till mixture resembles coarse crumbs. Add milk mixture to brown sugar mixture; beat well.

Line 9-inch pie plate with pastry. Pour in custard filling. Bake at 400° till knife inserted halfway between center and edge comes out clean, about 30 minutes. Cool. If desired, garnish with whipped cream.

Custard with extra flavor

←Coconut adds chewiness to creamy custard in Toasted Coconut Pie. Garnish with toasted coconut atop whipped cream wreath.

Custardy Rhubarb Pie

A scrumptious summertime dessert—

   1½ cups sugar
    ¼ cup all-purpose flour
    ¼ teaspoon ground nutmeg
        3 slightly beaten eggs
        1 pound rhubarb, cut in 1-inch
            slices (4 cups)

            •   •   •

            Plain Pastry for 9-inch lattice-
            top pie (See *Pastry*)
        2 tablespoons butter or margarine

Combine sugar, flour, and nutmeg; beat into eggs. Stir in sliced rhubarb. Line 9-inch pie plate with pastry. Fill with rhubarb mixture. Dot butter or margarine atop filling. Top with lattice crust; flute edge. Bake at 400° for 50 to 60 minutes. Cool.

Trifle Delight

Custard mix offers a quick variation of a favorite English dessert—

   2¼ cups milk
        1 2¾-ounce package no-bake
            vanilla custard mix

            •   •   •

        1 20½-ounce can pineapple tidbits,
            drained
        1 16-ounce can pitted dark sweet
            cherries, drained and halved
    ½ cup cream sherry

            •   •   •

        6 shortcake dessert cups *or* 6 slices
            pound cake

In small saucepan stir milk into vanilla custard mix; cook, stirring constantly, over high heat till mixture is boiling. Remove custard from heat; chill in the refrigerator.

In bowl combine drained pineapple tidbits, drained and halved cherries, and cream sherry. Chill fruit mixture 3 to 4 hours.

Drain chilled fruit mixture, reserving ¼ cup of the cream sherry. Beat custard smooth with rotary beater. Add reserved ¼ cup sherry; mix well. To serve, spoon chilled fruit onto shortcake dessert cups *or* pound cake slices; top with custard sauce. Makes 6 servings.

Delicately flavored Baked Custard makes an attractive dessert topped with tart jelly. Or, serve warm in cups with dash of nutmeg.

Baked Caramel Custard

    2 cups milk
    3 slightly beaten egg yolks
    2 slightly beaten eggs
    ½ cup sugar
    ½ teaspoon vanilla
        • • •
    ½ cup sugar

Scald milk over low heat; cool slightly. In bowl combine slightly beaten egg yolks, whole eggs, and ½ cup sugar; slowly stir in milk. Stir in vanilla; set mixture aside.

In heavy skillet stir ½ cup sugar over low heat till melted. When golden brown, remove from heat. Pour melted sugar into 1-quart casserole. Rotate casserole to coat sides with sugar syrup. Pour custard into casserole.

Set casserole in shallow baking pan on oven rack; pour hot water around casserole to depth of 1 inch. Bake at 325° till knife inserted halfway between center and edge comes out clean, about 1¼ hours. Chill. To serve, unmold onto serving platter. Makes 6 servings.

Baked Custard

    3 slightly beaten eggs
    ¼ cup sugar
    ¼ teaspoon salt
    2 cups milk, scalded and slightly
        cooled
    ½ teaspoon vanilla
        • • •
        Tart jelly (optional)
        Ground nutmeg (optional)

Combine eggs, sugar, and salt; slowly stir in milk and vanilla. Pour into six 5-ounce custard cups*. Set cups in shallow baking pan on oven rack. Pour hot water into pan to depth of 1 inch. Bake at 325° till knife inserted halfway between center and edge comes out clean, about 40 to 45 minutes. Serve warm; or, chill, unmold, and top with tart jelly or sprinkle with nutmeg. Makes 6 servings.

*For one large custard, bake the custard in a 1-quart casserole for about 60 minutes.

Caramel Custard Cups

Melt 12 vanilla caramels in ¼ cup milk over low heat, stirring constantly. Divide caramel sauce among six 5-ounce custard cups.

Prepare Baked Custard (see above); pour over sauce. Bake, following recipe directions. Serve warm, or chill and unmold. Serves 6.

Orange-Pumpkin Pudding

    3 slightly beaten eggs
    1 cup canned pumpkin
    ½ cup sugar
    ½ teaspoon ground cinnamon
    ¼ teaspoon ground allspice
    ¼ teaspoon grated orange peel
    1 14½-ounce can evaporated
        milk (1⅔ cups)

Combine first 6 ingredients; slowly stir in evaporated milk. Pour into six 5-ounce custard cups. Place in shallow baking pan; pour hot water around cups to depth of 1 inch. Bake at 325° till knife inserted halfway between center and edge comes out clean, about 50 minutes. Chill. Garnish with whipped cream and a sprinkle of ground cinnamon, if desired. Serves 6.

Cherry Bread Pudding

  2 cups milk
  3 slightly beaten eggs
  2 cups 1-inch day-old bread cubes
  ½ cup sugar
  ¼ teaspoon ground cinnamon
  1 teaspoon vanilla
  1 20-ounce can pitted tart red
    cherries (water pack)
  ½ cup sugar
  1 tablespoon cornstarch
    Few drops red food coloring
  2 to 3 drops almond extract
  ¼ cup flaked coconut, toasted

Combine milk and eggs; pour over bread cubes in mixing bowl. Stir in ½ cup sugar, cinnamon, vanilla, and ¼ teaspoon salt. Drain cherries, reserving syrup. Add *1 cup* of the drained cherries to bread mixture; toss lightly.

Spread mixture in greased 10x6x1¾-inch baking dish. Place dish in shallow baking pan on oven rack. Pour hot water around dish to depth of 1 inch. Bake at 350° till knife inserted halfway between center and edge comes out clean, about 40 to 45 minutes.

Meanwhile, add water to reserved cherry juice to make 1 cup. Combine ½ cup sugar and cornstarch in medium saucepan. Stir in cherry juice; cook and stir till thick and bubbly. Stir in remaining cherries, red food coloring, and almond extract; simmer 2 minutes longer.

To serve, sprinkle pudding with toasted coconut. Pass cherry sauce. Serves 8 or 9.

Pineapple-Cheese Parfaits

  1 2¾-ounce package no-bake
    vanilla custard mix
  2 cups milk
  2 3-ounce packages cream cheese,
    softened
  ½ teaspoon vanilla
  1 21-ounce can pineapple pie
    filling, chilled

Prepare custard according to package directions using the milk. Remove from heat. Gradually stir hot mixture into cheese; mix well. Stir in vanilla. Chill. To serve, spoon alternate layers of custard mixture and pie filling into parfait glasses. Makes 6 to 8 servings.

Zuppa Inglese

  6 egg yolks
  ½ cup cold water
  1½ cups granulated sugar
  ½ teaspoon vanilla
  ½ teaspoon orange *or* lemon
    extract
  1½ cups sifted cake flour
  ¼ teaspoon salt
  6 egg whites
  ¾ teaspoon cream of tartar
  ½ cup rum
  1 cup strawberry preserves

    · · ·

    Custard Filling
  1½ cups whipping cream
  1 teaspoon vanilla
  3 tablespoons confectioners'
    sugar
    Candied cherries

Beat egg yolks till thick and lemon-colored; add water. Beat till very thick, about 5 minutes. Gradually beat in granulated sugar, then ½ teaspoon vanilla and orange extract.

Sift flour with salt; fold into egg-yolk mixture a little at a time. Beat egg whites with cream of tartar till stiff peaks form. Carefully fold egg whites into cake mixture. Bake in *ungreased* 10-inch tube pan at 325° about 1 hour. Invert pan to cool.

When thoroughly cooled, remove from pan. Using wooden picks as a marking guide, split cake into 3 layers. Divide rum and sprinkle atop each layer. Place bottom layer on cake plate; spread with *half* of the preserves, then with *1 cup* of the Custard Filling.

Top with second layer. Spread with remaining preserves and Custard Filling. Top with remaining layer. Whip cream with 1 teaspoon vanilla and confectioners' sugar; frost entire cake. Garnish with candied cherries. Chill dessert thoroughly, about 3 to 4 hours.

Custard Filling: In saucepan combine ⅓ cup granulated sugar, 1 tablespoon all-purpose flour, 1 tablespoon cornstarch, and ¼ teaspoon salt. Gradually stir in 1½ cups milk. Cook and stir till thick and bubbly; cook and stir 2 to 3 minutes more. Stir a little of the hot mixture into 1 slightly beaten egg yolk; return to hot mixture. Bring just to boiling; stir constantly. Stir in 1 tablespoon butter or margarine, and 1 teaspoon vanilla. Cool.

Custard Pie

    4 slightly beaten eggs
    ½ cup sugar
    ½ teaspoon vanilla
    2½ cups milk, scalded and
        slightly cooled
       Plain Pastry for 1-crust 9-inch
        pie (See *Pastry*)

Blend first 3 ingredients and ¼ teaspoon salt. Slowly stir in milk. Line 9-inch pie plate with pastry. Pour filling into pastry-lined pie plate. Sprinkle with nutmeg, if desired.

Bake at 350° till knife inserted halfway between center and edge comes out clean, about 35 to 40 minutes. Serve cool or well chilled.

Slipped Custard Pie

Prepare filling for Custard Pie (above). Place buttered 8-inch pie plate in shallow baking pan. Fill pie plate with custard (pour extra into custard cups and bake with pie filling).

Fill pan with hot water. Bake at 350° till knife inserted halfway between center and edge comes out clean, 35 to 40 minutes. Cool. Run spatula around edge. Shake to loosen. Hold custard just above far rim of *baked* 9-inch pastry shell; gently slip into shell. Chill.

Potato-Cheese Custard

    2 cups raw, diced, peeled potato
         •   •   •
    2 cups milk
    1 5-ounce jar process cheese spread
        with bacon
    1 teaspoon instant minced onion
         •   •   •
    2 beaten eggs
    1 tablespoon snipped parsley
    ½ teaspoon salt
    ½ teaspoon dry mustard
       Dash pepper
       Bacon, crisp-cooked and
        crumbled

In saucepan add water to potatoes to cover; bring to boiling. Remove from heat; drain. Arrange potatoes in 10x6x1¾-inch baking dish.

In saucepan heat together milk, cheese spread, and instant minced onion, stirring occasionally till cheese melts. Meanwhile, in mixing bowl combine eggs, parsley, salt, dry mustard, and pepper. Gradually stir hot milk mixture into egg mixture; pour over potatoes.

Bake at 325° till knife inserted halfway between center and edge comes out clean, about 35 to 40 minutes. Top with crisp-cooked, crumbled bacon. Let casserole stand 5 minutes before serving. Makes 6 servings.

To avoid spills, place pastry-lined pie plate on oven rack. Pour in custard mixture, filling the pie plate just to fluted edge.

When custard-type pie or casserole mixture is done, knife inserted halfway between center and edge will come out clean.

Corn–Custard Casserole

- 1 10½-ounce can condensed cream of celery soup
- 2 tablespoons all-purpose flour
- 1 tablespoon prepared mustard
  Dash salt
- 1 12-ounce can whole kernel corn, undrained
- 1 6-ounce can evaporated milk (⅔ cup)
- 2 tablespoons chopped green pepper
- 2 tablespoons chopped onion
- 2 tablespoons chopped canned pimiento
- 2 slightly beaten eggs
- 1 teaspoon Worcestershire sauce

Blend cream of celery soup, flour, prepared mustard, and salt. Stir in undrained corn, evaporated milk, green pepper, onion, pimiento, beaten eggs, and Worcestershire sauce.

Turn mixture into 10x6x1¾-inch baking dish. Bake at 350° till knife inserted halfway between center and edge comes out clean, about 30 to 40 minutes. Makes 6 servings.

Herbed Spinach Bake

- 1 10-ounce package frozen chopped spinach
  . . .
- 1 cup cooked long-grain rice
- 4 ounces sharp process American cheese, shredded (1 cup)
- 2 slightly beaten eggs
- ⅓ cup milk
- 2 tablespoons butter or margarine, softened
- 2 tablespoons chopped onion
- 1 teaspoon salt
- ½ teaspoon Worcestershire sauce
- ¼ teaspoon dried rosemary leaves, crushed, *or* dried thyme leaves, crushed

Cook spinach according to package directions; drain. Stir in remaining ingredients. Pour mixture into 10x6x1¾-inch baking dish. Bake at 350° till knife inserted halfway between center and edge comes out clean, 20 to 25 minutes. Cut in squares to serve. Serves 6.

Swiss and Crab Pie

- Plain Pastry for 1-crust 9-inch pie (See *Pastry*)
- 4 ounces natural Swiss cheese, shredded (1 cup)
- 1 7½-ounce can crab meat, drained, flaked, and cartilage removed
- 2 green onions with tops, sliced
- 3 beaten eggs
- 1 cup light cream
- ½ teaspoon salt
- ½ teaspoon grated lemon peel
- ¼ teaspoon dry mustard
  Dash ground mace
- ¼ cup sliced almonds

Line 9-inch pie plate with pastry. Sprinkle cheese over bottom of unbaked shell. Top with crab; sprinkle with onions. Combine remaining ingredients except almonds. Pour mixture over crab. Sprinkle with almonds. Bake at 325° till knife inserted halfway between center and edge comes out clean, about 45 minutes. Remove from oven; let stand 10 minutes. Serves 6.

Onion Pie

- 1 cup finely crushed saltine crackers (28 crackers)
- ¼ cup butter or margarine, melted
  . . .
- 2 cups thinly sliced onion, separated into rings (2 medium)
- 2 tablespoons butter or margarine
- ¾ cup milk
- 2 slightly beaten eggs
- ¼ cup shredded sharp process American cheese
  Dash paprika

Mix crumbs with ¼ cup melted butter. Press onto bottom and sides of 8-inch pie plate.

Cook onion in 2 tablespoons butter till tender but not brown; place in crumb shell. Combine milk, eggs, ¾ teaspoon salt, and dash pepper; pour over onions. Sprinkle pie with cheese and paprika. Bake at 350° till knife inserted halfway between center and edge comes out clean, about 30 minutes. Garnish with additional cooked onion rings and parsley, if desired. Serve hot. Makes 4 to 6 main dish servings, or 10 to 12 appetizers.

Snow Pudding

¾ cup sugar
¼ teaspoon salt
1 envelope unflavored gelatin
   (1 tablespoon)
½ cup cold water

. . .

¾ cup cold water
1 teaspoon grated lemon peel
¼ cup lemon juice
2 egg whites

. . .

3 egg yolks *or* 1 whole egg plus
   2 egg yolks
3 tablespoons sugar
Dash salt
1½ cups milk, scalded and slightly
   cooled
1 teaspoon vanilla
Tart red jelly

In small saucepan combine ¾ cup sugar, ¼ teaspoon salt, and unflavored gelatin. Add the ½ cup cold water. Cook over low heat, stirring constantly, till gelatin dissolves.

Remove from heat; stir in ¾ cup cold water, lemon peel, and lemon juice. Chill till partially set. Turn into large mixing bowl. Add egg whites. Beat with electric or rotary beater till mixture begins to hold its shape.

Turn pudding mixture into eight 5-ounce custard cups. Chill till pudding is firm.

To make sauce, beat 3 egg yolks *or* 1 whole egg plus 2 egg yolks in top of double boiler. Add 3 tablespoons sugar and dash salt.

Gradually stir in slightly cooled milk. Cook and stir over hot, *not boiling*, water till mixture coats a metal spoon. Remove from heat; cool at once by placing pan in bowl of cold water and stirring a minute or two. Stir in vanilla; chill custard sauce.

Just before serving, unmold snow puddings into serving dish. Ladle some custard sauce over puddings; dot with tart, red jelly. Pass remaining custard sauce. Makes 8 servings.

Golden custard sauce

Drizzle creamy custard sauce atop airy puffs of Snow Pudding. Tart, red jelly adds the crowning touch to this delicate dessert.

CUSTARD APPLE—The name given to several fruits of various tropical and subtropical shrubs or small trees. The fruit most commonly termed custard apple has a dark brown surface marked with depressions, giving it a quilted appearance. The pulp is reddish yellow with a very soft texture—thus, the name. It has a sweet flavor, yet is very bland, which contributes to its popularity in hot climates. Other fruits closely related to custard apple include cherimoya, sweetsop, and soursop.

CUT IN—To mix solid shortening or butter with dry ingredients using a pastry blender or two knives. Ingredients should be evenly and finely divided.

CUTLERY—Sharp-edged cutting utensils or tools, such as knives and kitchen shears, used for slicing, peeling, chopping, coring, boning, or trimming in the preparation of food. (See *Kitchen Shears, Knife* for additional information.)

CUTLET—1. A thin slice of meat, especially veal, mutton, or pork cut from the leg and cooked by broiling or frying. Formerly, a cutlet was cut from the rib section of the animal. 2. A flat croquette made of minced meat or fish, shaped to resemble a meat cutlet. (See also *Veal.*)

Veal Parmigiano

Melt 3 tablespoons butter or margarine in 10x6x1¾-inch baking dish. Combine ½ cup cornflake crumbs, ¼ cup grated Parmesan cheese, ½ teaspoon salt, and dash pepper.

Cut 1 pound veal cutlets, about ¼ inch thick, into 4 serving-size pieces. Dip in 1 slightly beaten egg, then in cornflake crumb mixture. Place cutlets in baking dish. Bake at 400° for 20 minutes. Turn cutlets; bake till tender, about 15 to 20 minutes longer.

Meanwhile, in saucepan combine one 8-ounce can tomato sauce; ½ teaspoon dried oregano leaves, crushed; ½ teaspoon sugar; and dash onion salt. Heat mixture to boiling, stirring frequently. Pour tomato sauce mixture over cooked cutlets. Arrange 4 ounces sliced mozzarella cheese atop meat. Return casserole to oven to melt cheese. Makes 4 servings.

Fondue Veal Strips

   1½ pounds veal cutlets
   ¼ cup all-purpose flour
   2 beaten eggs
   ½ cup fine dry bread crumbs
     Salad oil
     Horseradish Sauce
     Mustard Sauce

Pound veal to ⅛-inch thickness. Cut in 3x1-inch strips. Coat strips with mixture of flour and ¼ teaspoon salt, then dip in egg. Roll in bread crumbs. Loosely thread each strip accordion-fashion on bamboo skewer.

Pour salad oil into metal fondue cooker to ½ capacity. Heat to 425° on range (do not let oil smoke). Add 1 teaspoon salt to hot oil. Place cooker over fondue burner. Let each guest fry veal strips in hot oil till browned. Dip in assorted sauces. Makes 4 servings.

Horseradish Sauce: Whip one 8-ounce package softened cream cheese with 2 to 3 tablespoons prepared horseradish till fluffy. Chill.

Mustard Sauce: Combine 1 cup dairy sour cream, ¼ cup milk, 3 tablespoons dry onion soup mix, and 2 tablespoons prepared mustard. Heat and stir, but do not boil. Serve hot.

Veal Bertrand

   6 veal cutlets (about 2 pounds)
   ⅔ cup dry sherry
   1 6-ounce can whole mushrooms, drained
   ¼ cup snipped parsley
     Dash garlic powder
   6 tablespoons butter or margarine
   3 slices process Swiss cheese

Pound veal cutlets to ¼-inch thickness. Combine sherry, drained mushrooms, parsley, and garlic powder. Pour over veal. Marinate 30 minutes, turning several times.

Melt butter in skillet. Drain meat, reserving marinade. Quickly cook *half* of the meat in hot butter, about 3 minutes on each side. Remove from skillet; repeat with remaining meat. Return cooked meat to skillet; add reserved marinade. Bring to boiling; reduce heat. Arrange cheese slices over meat. Cover; heat just till cheese melts. Remove to warm platter; spoon sauce atop meat. Makes 6 servings.

The cutting board is a most versatile piece of kitchen equipment. Choose a size appropriate for the amount of cutting to be done.

The recipe which follows illustrates the "croquette" definition of the word "cutlet." The patty shape gives interesting and appealing menu variation for this breaded meat mixture.

Polish Cutlets

    ¼ cup milk
    ¼ cup butter or margarine,
        melted
    1 cup soft bread crumbs
        (about 1½ slices)
    ½ teaspoon lemon juice
    ½ teaspoon salt
    ½ teaspoon paprika
        Dash pepper
    1½ pounds ground veal
            • • •
    1 beaten egg
    2 tablespoons water
    ½ cup fine dry bread crumbs
    2 tablespoons shortening
        Gravy

Combine milk, butter, soft bread crumbs, lemon juice, salt, paprika, and pepper; add veal and mix well. Form meat mixture into 6 patties, ¾ inch thick. Combine egg with water; dip patties into egg mixture, then dip into dry bread crumbs. In skillet brown patties on both sides in hot shortening. Simmer, covered, till meat is done, about 15 to 20 minutes.

To prepare *Gravy:* Remove patties to warm platter. Pour off pan drippings, reserving 1 tablespoon. To reserved drippings in skillet, blend in 1 tablespoon all-purpose flour, ¼ teaspoon ground nutmeg, ¼ teaspoon salt, and dash pepper. Add 1 cup milk all at once. Cook, stirring constantly, till mixture thickens and bubbles. Stir in 1 teaspoon lemon juice. Serve with patties. Makes 6 servings.

CUTTING BOARD—A smooth, hardwood board used for slicing, cutting, mincing, or chopping foods. Cutting board sizes vary greatly. Small ones are used for a small amount of food preparation; larger boards, either portable or built into the counter, are suitable for larger quantities.

With some exacting care, cutting boards can provide long, sanitary service. The application of several coatings of hot salad oil improves sanitation by sealing the wood pores. After using a board, wash and dry it. As an additional health precaution and as prevention against warped wood, don't allow the board to rest in the sink while other food preparation goes on.

CUTTLEFISH—A 10-armed saltwater mollusk similar to squid or octopus. It differs from them by having a calcified internal shell called the cuttlebone.

This seafood is common to Grecian, Indian, Italian, Japanese, and Spanish diets. The meat is edible only after being made sufficiently tender by beating. It is then cooked like octopus. (See *Octopus, Squid* for additional information.)

CYDER—The British spelling for the alcoholic beverage, cider. (See also *Cider*.)

CYMLING SQUASH—Another name for pattypan squash, a summer variety identified by its shape—scalloped, flat, and dishlike. (See also *Pattypan Squash*.)

D

DAB — 1. A very small portion of food, for example, a small dollop of jam used to garnish a cookie. 2. The name of a flatfish related to the flounder family. These fish are found off the North American and European coasts of the North Atlantic Ocean as well as in the Pacific Ocean. Dabs are lean fish with a distinctive flavor and a delicate texture. The flesh tastes slightly sweet but is not oily. A comparatively thick layer of flesh on either side of the backbone is delightfully free from bones. Dabs can be panfried like other types of panfish. (See also *Flounder*.)

DACE — A small, silvery fish of both European and North American fresh waters. Dace belong to the carp family.

Dace flesh is tough but completely edible. These fish are usually fried in the same way as are smelts. (See *Carp, Smelt* for additional information.)

DAFFODIL CAKE — A light and delicate foam-type cake that was originally a combination of angel food (made with egg whites) and sponge cake (made with egg yolks). Daffodil cake takes it name from the attractive intermingling of white and yellow colors throughout the cake. A quick, easy way to produce the same effect in a delicious cake is given here in the cake mix-base recipe Easy Daffodil Cake.

Easy Daffodil Cake

A subtle merger of yellow and white captures that springtime feeling—

> 1 package angel cake mix
> 1 teaspoon water
> ¼ teaspoon yellow food coloring
>
> . . .
>
> 2 egg whites
> 1 cup sugar
> 2 tablespoons lemon juice
> ¼ teaspoon cream of tartar
>   Dash salt
> 1 cup miniature marshmallows
> ½ teaspoon grated lemon peel

Prepare angel cake mix according to package directions; divide batter in half. Combine water and yellow food coloring; fold into *half* the batter. Spoon colored and plain cake batters alternately into *ungreased* 10-inch tube pan. Bake as directed on package. Invert cake in pan; cool the cake thoroughly.

Meanwhile, prepare lemon frosting by combining egg whites, sugar, lemon juice, cream of tartar, and salt in top of double boiler. Beat mixture for 1 minute with electric or rotary beater. Cook over boiling water, beating till stiff peaks form. Carefully fold in miniature marshmallows and lemon peel.

When cake is cool, remove from pan. Frost sides and top with lemon frosting.

DAIKON *(dī' kan)* — A large white radish, available throughout the year, which is eaten raw by the Chinese, Japanese, and the Koreans. This heavy, root vegetable may grow to be three feet long, six inches thick, and weigh up to fifty pounds. Imported from Hawaii or Japan, it can be found in the Western states in one of three forms: oblong, spherical, or cylindrical. The small oblong radish, generally four inches long and three inches thick, is the favorite of the Chinese. The Japanese favor the larger and longer spherical and cylindrical varieties of daikon.

The Oriental radish has a somewhat more spongy texture than the Western radish, but the flavor is similar. The vivid, green radish foliage is sought after as a special green vegetable by cultivating the daikon seedlings. A long, slender white taproot is tied around bunches of twenty or more plants and sold in markets.

To non-Oriental cooks, daikon is best known in preserved versions of vegetables pickled in soy sauce, seaweed derivatives, and other flavorings. Well chilled, thinly sliced, pickled daikon is an essential item for those serving Oriental menus. The root is often carved into a variety of shapes, such as roses or fishnets, for garnishes. Shredded, raw daikon may be used as a bed for Nipponese raw fish or as a Suki-yaki condiment. It may also be mixed in with warm soy sauce dip. Pickled daikon can be paired with American hamburgers and hot dogs for an unusual accompaniment. (See *Japanese Cookery, Radish* for additional information.)

DAIQUIRI *(dī' karē, dak' uh rē)* — A tart cocktail made of white rum, lime juice, and sugar shaken with finely shaven ice. The cocktail, named after a mining town in southeastern Cuba where American troops landed after the Spanish-American War, is popular as a summer drink.

The ingredients, white rum (preferred because of delicate flavor), lime juice, and sugar, are poured over finely shaven ice and shaken or blended just until the drink is thoroughly chilled—too much shaking or blending will cause the ice to dissolve and dilute the cocktail. To produce an even foamier daiquiri, add a dash of egg white to the mixing glass just before shaking. Make two or three small fresh cocktails in a shaker at a time for maximum flavor. The classic daiquiri is sometimes strained to remove small ice particles which cause dilution. Pour the iced drink into a chilled cocktail glass. You may add a lime slice or wedge and serve along with a short straw. The cocktail is to be sipped slowly.

A frozen daiquiri is prepared the same way, but the mixture is combined with crushed ice in an electric blender and blended until it looks like snow. Interesting daiquiri variations can be prepared by adding fresh or frozen orange juice or chopped peaches to the standard mixture before blending. (See also *Cocktail.*)

Daiquiri

Combine ½ jigger lime juice, 1 jigger (1½ ounces) light rum, powdered sugar to taste, 1 teaspoon Triple Sec (optional), and crushed ice in a shaker. Shake well and strain into a stemmed cocktail glass. Makes 1 cocktail.

DAIRY SOUR CREAM — A commercial dairy product sold in American markets and produced by a culture of lactic acid bacteria acting upon sweet light cream.

Pasteurization and homogenization processes assure even fat distribution before the addition of the lactic acid bacteria to the cream. The cream, then, is subjected to proper temperatures for a measured length of time and then chilled to stop the bacteria action. The cream is packaged as commercial dairy sour cream and is uniform in texture at all times.

When dairy sour cream is exposed to high cooking temperatures, curdling may occur. In certain cases, holding it at a low temperature for a longer length of time may also produce the same reaction. To avoid this keep the temperature low and usually add the dairy sour cream near the end of the cooking time when using in most cooked dishes. The curdling, however, only affects the appearance and not the flavor. Smooth, thick dairy sour cream is used in dips, soups, main dishes, desserts, and cakes. (See also *Sour Cream.*)

DAMPF NOODLE—A yeast dumpling served with stewed fruit, jam, or a sauce. These German dumplings, or *dampfnudeln,* are shaped from dough which has been enriched with sugar, eggs, and butter.

The small, round biscuitlike balls are placed in a baking dish and allowed to rise. They are parboiled (boiled for a short time; not cooked completely) in milk, then steamed and browned in the oven.

These dumplings can be arranged on a heated platter or individual serving dishes with a sauce spooned over them. Sauce suggestions include hot vanilla sauce, caramel, or dried fruit sauce.

DAMSON PLUMS *(dam' zen)*—A small bluish purple plum eaten fresh or used in preserves. The plums were cultivated more than 2000 years ago in Damascus, Syria, where the plum's name originated. Today they are cultivated in tree orchards and also grow wild. The firm, oval plums are available from May through September.

Damson should be selected at their peak of ripeness. Look for full bluish purple color, firm plumpness, smooth skin, and fresh appearance. For canning purposes choose mellow plums not quite ripe. An excellent fruit for cooking, Damson plums may be used for jams, jellies, pickles, preserves, puddings, and pies. (See also *Plum.*)

DANDELION—A delectable spring green of the chicory family cultivated for its bitter, toothed or pinnated leaves which are used as a vegetable and in salads, and the roots used for wine and coffee. The sharply indented leaves influenced the French name *dent de lion* or "lion's tooth."

Grown and used not only in the United States, but in France, England, and Italy as well, the dandelion plant grows in the poorest soil and should not be picked before the yellow flower appears.

Two types of dandelions, cultivated and wild, are found on the market in early spring. Cultivated dandelions, with a bleached appearance, are more tender.

Select both types of dandelion greens carefully, avoiding the slightest bit of yellow bud as this causes an undesirable acrid taste. Choose young plants with tender, delicately flavored leaves.

Prepare the greens for cooking or for use in salads by first removing the root and quartering the base of the plant with a knife. Sand may be found among the leaves, so a thorough washing and cleaning is important. Drain and crisp the greens for salads in the refrigerator.

If the dandelion is to be used as a vegetable, it is cooked like spinach. Add dandelion greens to a small amount of salted water in saucepan and cook till completely wilted. Drain and discard the water which will have become quite strong. Formerly, boiling the greens for a long time with several changes of water was recommended to remove bitterness. Today, however, authorities say that this process results in a loss of the rich vitamin and mineral nutritive value of the vegetable greens.

The humble dandelion may be served raw, eaten as a vegetable, or made into several unique beverages. Pour a tart French dressing over a dandelion salad of thinly sliced scallions, radishes, and cooked beets. Cook the greens like spinach and serve with a creamy sauce. Dried, ground dandelion roots make a delicious European coffee substitute, and the flowers make a delectable wine. Dandelions are made into refreshing European and Oriental soups, and are blended in with fritters and omelets. (See also *Vegetable.*)

DANISH BLUE CHEESE—A pungent, blue-veined mold-ripened cheese made with homogenized milk, very rich in cream. Danish Blue Cheese can be recognized by its off-white color with blue green mold and a buttery paste consistency. This cheese was invented in 1914 by a Danish cheese-maker, Marius Boel, who produced a mold on a barley bread baked for that purpose.

The rich, creamy milk from which Danish Blue Cheese is made accounts for its buttery consistency. Roquefort, Norwegian, and other domestic blues contain less fat than the buttery Danish blue. The liberal number of penlike blue vein markings make this rich-flavored cheese look like a delicate work of art. The cheeses made for local Danish consumption are lower in cream content, even more densely veined, and are sharper in flavor with a slight peppermint taste. (See also Blue *Cheese.*)

DANISH COOKERY—Food and drink influenced by the southernmost Scandinavian country—Denmark. Foods characteristic of this land of rich agricultural heritage and abundance include tiny artistic open-face sandwiches, buttery-rich pastries and desserts, steaming loaves of yeast bread, ground fish dishes, flavorful meatballs, fruit soups, and rice porridge. Rich foods, such as butter, cream, and eggs, are used lavishly in preparing dishes to satisfy the hearty appetites of Danish eaters.

Traditional recipes, handed down for generations, are the basis for Danish cuisine. Some are simple country-style recipes, while others, tinged with French cooking, are more sophisticated. The thrifty Danes treat their food with respect, as every scrap finds its way into a delectable dish such as open-faced sandwiches.

A Danish open-face sandwich is a small sandwich, or *Smörrebröd* of thinly sliced buttered bread topped with the main ingredient, artistically arranged, and tastefully garnished. The sandwich can be found almost anywhere in Denmark and is sold on street corners, boats, trains, and in restaurants. One restaurant has a yard-long menu listing some 175 choices.

The bread is usually buttered and may be white, rye, or a crisp bread. The main ingredient is carefully arranged and garnished keeping texture and color in mind. A leaf green is sometimes tucked under a filling corner. The lovely little meal is eaten with a knife and a fork.

Shrimp-Capers Sandwich

For each sandwich, butter 1 slice French bread generously. Cover with a ruffly leaf of lettuce. Arrange canned tiny shrimp, overlapping, in two rows atop lettuce. Pipe mayonnaise or salad dressing from pastry tube down sandwich center. Top with capers.

Danish open-face sandwiches

←Artistic Danish cookery consists of an open-face sandwich buffet of Shrimp-Capers, Ham Pinwheel, and Egg-Sardine-Tomato.

Ham Pinwheel Sandwiches

    8 slices whole wheat bread
    ⅓ cup mayonnaise or salad
         dressing
    1⅓ cups shredded lettuce
    1 3-ounce package cream cheese,
         softened
    1 teaspoon horseradish
    4 slices Danish-style boiled ham

Spread bread with mayonnaise; top with shredded lettuce. Blend cream cheese and horseradish, adding milk if necessary to make mixture of spreading consistency. Spread evenly on ham slices. Roll up tightly. (To make slicing easier, refrigerate the rolls a short time.) Slice each ham roll into tiny pinwheels. Arrange pinwheels on shredded lettuce in diagonal line, 5 per sandwich. Makes 8 sandwiches.

Egg-Tomato-Sardine Sandwiches

Butter 1 slice rye bread generously for each sandwich. Mix chopped hard-cooked egg with mayonnaise or salad dressing to moisten; spread on buttered bread. Arrange canned sardines and small tomato wedges atop egg. Garnish with parsley or dill sprigs.

In this dairy country excellent cheeses are made and enjoyed in every possible way. Cream is used generously in cooking, and butter is the shortening used in most baked foods. Buttermilk soup, delectably flavored with sugar, raisins, and lemon peel, is enriched with cream. Salads are preferred with a sour cream sauce, vegetables are usually served with a cream sauce, and whipped cream is used to top puddings, cakes, and desserts.

The Danish also are great lovers of rye breads. Hearty white and satisfying dark rye Danish breads are integral parts of meal courses. Rye bread crusts are used with beer in a simple brown soup. Rye bread crumbs, with milk and sugar, are used in an apple whipped cream dessert garnished with grated chocolate. World famous Danish coffee bread, *Wienerbröd* (Vienna bread), is produced by steaming the yeast loaves in the oven while baking.

Danish Coffee Ring

Tender Danish pastry ring with sugar icing and raisin-nut filling—

    1 package active dry yeast
2½ to 3 cups sifted all-purpose flour
    ¾ cup milk, scalded
    ¼ cup shortening
    ¼ cup sugar
    ½ teaspoon salt

• • •

    1 slightly beaten egg
    ½ teaspoon vanilla
    1 teaspoon grated lemon peel

• • •

    2 tablespoons butter, melted
    ½ cup raisins
    ½ cup slivered almonds, toasted
    ⅓ cup sugar
    ½ teaspoon ground mace *or*
        1½ teaspoons ground cinnamon
    Icing

In large bowl combine yeast and 1½ *cups* flour. Heat milk, shortening, sugar, and ½ teaspoon salt just till warm, stirring occasionally to melt shortening. Add to dry mixture in bowl; add egg, vanilla, and lemon peel. Beat at low speed with electric mixer for ½ minute, scraping sides of bowl constantly. Beat 3 minutes at high speed. By hand, stir in enough of remaining flour to make soft dough.

Knead on floured surface till smooth and elastic. Place in greased bowl, turning once to grease surface of dough. Cover and let rest till double, about 1½ hours. Punch down. Cover and let rest 10 minutes. Roll to 21x7 inches, ¼ inch thick. (Or, divide dough in half and roll to 13x6 inches to make two smaller rings.)

A Danish Kringle becomes a special treat for family and friends when stuffed with a sweet and spicy raisin or pecan filling. Serve the flaky coffee bread, adorned with toasted almond pieces, with tiny butter curls and steaming hot cups of coffee.

Brush dough with melted butter. Combine remaining ingredients; spread on dough. Roll from long edge; seal. Shape ring on greased baking sheet. With scissors, snip almost to center at 1-inch intervals. Pull sections apart; twist slightly. Cover, let rise till double, about 50 minutes. Bake at 375° for 20 minutes. Frost with *Icing:* Mix 1 cup sifted confectioners' sugar, 4 teaspoons milk, ½ teaspoon vanilla, and dash salt. Makes 1 large ring.

As befits a country of many islands and available fresh fish markets, the Danish are great fishermen and are fond of fish dishes. Ground white fish baked with bread crumbs may be served to the family hot at dinner time, or sliced and served cold at a buffet party with garnishes of sliced hard-cooked eggs, tomatoes, cucumber, and dill. Skinned eel, and other such seafoods, may be jellied with carrots and peppercorns or fried in butter and served with apple-curry sauce or other such accompaniments.

Danish cooks make ground beef, veal, or pork into flavorful meatballs called *Frikadeller*. Similar mixtures may be the stuffing for cabbage or the heart of broth cooked dumplings. Fresh pork is delectably stuffed with prunes and apples for roasting, chicken is often stuffed with a handful of parsley, and the Christmas roast goose has a stuffing of prunes. Also at holiday times, a reindeer roast, imported from Iceland, may be the special treat.

Pickling, a meat preservation technique of the past, is now an important flavor addition. Pickled duck served with horseradish cream sauce is one such specialty.

Traditional in Denmark is a rice porridge, served piping hot with a chunk of cold butter in the center. At Christmas time it is a "must," served with sugar, cinnamon, and cream. Typically Danish, too, are the dainty apple puffs called *Abelskiver*, baked in a special iron utensil with numerous rounded cups. As in other Scandinavian countries, fruit soups are made in Denmark and often are served as a dessert. Danish cooks are experts at making thin, dainty pancakes to be served with a filling of rich ice cream or cool fruit. (See *Danish Pastry, Scandinavian Cookery* for additional information.)

DANISH HAM—An imported specialty ham weighing up to 12 to 14 pounds. These boneless, fully cooked hams are packed in cans and weigh from 1½ to 6 or 7 pounds or are marketed in 4- to 6-ounce packages. These hams come from animals that have been fed on a milk and grain diet, the reason for the tender, succulent, juicy meat.

As with all fully cooked hams, Danish hams may be thinly sliced, or baked to heat through, garnished, and served hot or cold. Uniformly sliced, fully cooked Danish ham is available in 4- to 6-ounce packets in markets. (See also *Ham.*)

DANISH PASTRY—Traditional Danish sweet, buttery-rich, yeast-raised rolls and coffee cakes. Dough is spread with chilled butter or margarine and folded into three layers and rolled. The technique is similar to puff pastry. Fillings of dried fruit, jelly, or soft cheese are placed in the center. Delightful individual pastries or masterfully shaped large, holiday breads can be formed from the rich dough. Occasionally the dough is chilled before baking, and an egg and water mixture is brushed on the raised surface to give it a glazed appearance.

As part of the cooking process, the delicate pastries are sometimes put into a preheated hot oven, which is reduced quickly to moderate to bake evenly. Mouth-watering garnishes and flavor additions, such as sugar, candied fruits, nuts, spices, and icing add the finishing touch. (See also *Scandinavian Cookery.*)

Danish Kringle

Roll ¾ cup softened butter or margarine out between two sheets of wax paper to 10x6-inch rectangle. Chill. Soften 1 package active dry yeast in ¼ cup *warm* water. Combine 1 slightly beaten egg, ¼ cup sugar, 1 teaspoon salt, and ¾ cup cold milk in large mixing bowl. Stir in softened yeast and 3 cups sifted all-purpose flour. Mix well to form a moderately stiff dough. Roll dough out on a lightly floured surface to a 12-inch square.

Place chilled butter in center of dough square. Overlap dough; pinch to seal center seam and ends. Cover and let rest 10 minutes. Roll out again to 12-inch square. Fold in thirds. Wrap in foil and chill 30 to 60 minutes; repeat rolling, chilling and folding twice more. Cut dough lengthwise into 3 strips, 12-inches long. Roll first strip out to an 18x4-inch rectangle. Combine 1 beaten egg with 1 tablespoon water; brush on strip with pastry brush. Sprinkle strip with ⅓ of the Sweet Filling. Seal edges together to form 18-inch long roll. Shape into an oval, placing seam side down in greased baking sheet.

Seal ends together and flatten dough with rolling pin or palm of hand to ½-inch thickness. Brush flattened surface with remaining egg-water mixture. Using ¼ cup finely chopped blanched almonds and ¼ cup sugar, sprinkle a third over the top. Repeat with remaining dough, filling, and topping. Let dough rest at room temperature for 30 minutes. Bake at 375° till golden brown, about 25 minutes. Remove to rack; cool. Makes 3 kringles.

Sweet filling: In small bowl cream together ½ cup butter or margarine and 1½ cups sugar till fluffy. Stir in 1½ cups golden raisins or 1½ cups coarsely chopped pecans.

DARJEELING TEA (*där je′ ling*)—A variety of black tea grown at altitudes of from 1,000 to 7,000 feet in the Himalaya Mountains near Darjeeling, India. Considered to be India's finest tea, its pungent, distinctive flavor permeates the flavor of other teas. This black tea is blended into many American tea brands for that reason. Prized as a "straight" brew, Darjeeling tea produces an attractive, handsome reddish color when brewed. (See also *Tea*.)

DASHEEN (*da shēn′*)—A starchy root vegetable grown in southern United States and in tropical climates as a substitute for potatoes. A variety of taro, it has grown as a commercial crop in the Southern states since 1913. The nutlike-flavored vegetable grows in a warmer, more moist climate than does the potato and is a staple food for the people of southeastern Asia, Polynesia, an the Pacific Islands.

The vegetable consists of one large bulbous root with many smaller attached tubers. The larger root, called the corm, can weigh up to 6 pounds. The light tan vegetable is characterized by heavy, circumference rings; shaggy, fibrous skin; and a tapering, round, stem end. The small roots called tubers or cormels, often irregular in shape, may be cream-colored or run from gray to lavender shades.

Being a starch tuber, the dasheen has more carbohydrates and proteins than do potatoes and is easily digested. The roots are most readily available in Spanish neighborhoods in vegetable shops.

When purchasing dasheens, select a heavy, full-bodied vegetable with a firm, fresh-looking skin. It will keep 4 to 5 days if it is stored in a cool, dark, well-ventilated storage place.

Before cooking, scrub, but do not peel the vegetable as its raw juice irritates the skin. They should then be cooked like potatoes in boiling salted water until tender, usually about 15 to 30 minutes. After cooking they should be peeled and mashed or put through a ricer. Season cooked dasheens with salt and pepper to taste and plenty of butter or margarine.

Dasheens may be baked by first boiling and then adding a thin oil coat to prevent a hard rind. Hollow out corm interior. Par-boil hollowed dasheens for 10 minutes in salted water, and stuff with meat, fish, or green vegetables. Slice raw dasheens and onions in greased baking dish, sprinkle with cheese and buttered crumbs, and bake. Prepare a pie filling of boiled, riced dasheens with butter, sugar, egg, milk, and spices. Drop dasheen fritters in hot fat, sprinkling with powdered sugar after cooking. Any potato recipe may be used for this potato substitute if the homemaker remembers that dasheens need added moisture and fat because they are drier than are potatoes. (See also *Taro*.)

DATE—A one-seeded berry fruit growing in thick clusters on a tall date palm tree. Dates are sweet and flavorful, plump and lustrous, golden brown to deep amber in color, and smooth skinned.

In its long history dating back more than 8000 years to Mesopotamia (now Iraq) in an area commonly associated with the Garden of Eden, the brown fruit has had many uses. It has been used as a fruit, to make bread and wine, and has saved many a wanderer in the deserts of the Middle East and Africa from starvation.

Records show that the Egyptian queen, Cleopatra, ate dates and drank wine made from them. A kind of bread containing dates was also eaten by the Egyptians and the Greeks. Greeks dedicated the date to the god of music and poetry because it was thought of as a symbol of light, fertility, and riches. The plump dates were favorite sweets in Ancient Persia, and palm branches became symbolic of Jesus' march to Jerusalem on Palm Sunday.

Had it not been for dates and their ability to thrive in hot, dry climates, the desert populations and camels of the Middle East and Africa might not have survived the torrid climate. Fortunately, the sight of a palm tree offered welcome shade relief and food to the people who lived in or traveled through the scorching hot and barren desert countries.

Because of the abundance of dates in these desert regions, the fruit has become a principal source of wealth in those countries where they grow abundantly.

Early Spanish missionaries introduced dates to the Western world. Some of the original palm offshoots may still be found in parts of Southern California and Mexico where their missions were first established. The Department of Agriculture, in 1890, shipped in date varieties from Egypt. Commercial firm representatives began visiting date growing countries bringing back better shoots from the date palms. By the middle of the nineteenth century, a climate best suited for large-scale production of dates was found to be the warm valleys of California and Arizona. Today, California and Arizona are still America's leading date-producing states. Dates are also grown in Texas, Florida, and the Gulf States, but the fruit does not ripen as well in these states as it does in the climatic conditions of California and Arizona.

How dates are produced: The slender trunked date palm may reach a height of a hundred feet and have 10- to 20-foot long leaves that grow into a stiff, green crown. Palm trees must be hand-pollinated as the female blossoms have no scent to attract bees. The date clusters may weigh from 15 to 25 pounds and produce over 1000 dates. Date palms bear 300 to 400 pounds of fruit per season for one or two centuries. This long-lived tree, sometimes existing for more than 200 years, requires a hot climate and low humidity.

Dates begin to ripen during the late summer and early fall. The green, unripe dates are crisp, smooth, firm, and astringent. Mature size and full sugar content is attained before it turns to a red or yellow colored (depending on variety), sweet, thick-fleshed fruit. The date ripens to a glossy brown and the flesh softens and partially dries. Curing, the natural process of drying out, occurs as the fruit ripens.

Because the individual fruits do not ripen at the same time, harvesting usually continues from September through February. The ripe dates should be picked several times during the growing season to insure prime ripeness and proper curing. Trees are covered for protection from rain, birds, and insects during ripening.

Nutritional value: Dates have differing characteristics. The oblong fruit varies in shape, size, color, quality, and flesh consistency according to variety and environmental conditions. Age and ripeness of the fruit when picked determine the composition. Because dates are 60 to 65 percent sugar, they are high in calories and often are called "candy that grows on trees." Nutritionally valuable, dates contain vitamin A, some of the B vitamins, and are a good source for minerals—calcium, iron, phosphorus, and copper.

Kinds of dates: Dates are classified commercially as soft, semidry, and dry, depending upon the softness of the ripe fruit. They are also classified according to sugar content. Soft varieties are invert-sugar dates (containing mostly dextrose and levulose) and dry varieties are cane-sugar dates (containing mostly cane sugar). Semidry varieties may contain either.

Common invert-sugar soft varieties include Hayany, Barhee, Khadrawy, Rhars, Kustawy, Halawy, Sayer, Saidy, and Maktoom. The common cane-sugar dry dates include Kenta and Thoory. Semidry varieties include Zahidi and Deglet Noor. Deglet Noor is a cane-sugar date and Zahidi an invert-sugar type.

The nonperishable dry varieties contain very little moisture when ripe. Soft varieties are dehydrated after being sized and separated to bring them to the desired moisture content. Semidry dates are sold in their natural state as fresh dates.

The most popular date variety grown in the Coachella Valley of California is the semidry Deglet Noor, a native of Algeria. Other leading varieties of dates grown and used in the United States are the Egyptian Khadrawy, Zahidi, and Halawy.

How to select: Even though the date harvest season is from September through February, refrigeration makes it possible for dates to be available all year long. They are most plentiful around holiday seasons. Choose the black, sweet, meaty, thin-skinned date or the golden brown date with a coarse texture and larger seed.

Dates are sold pitted or unpitted in assorted sizes in overwrapped paper trays, jars, and film bags. As a convenience item, chopped or diced dates are also available. Regular and spiced dates, and canned date nut rolls are available in most markets and gift and mail order shops.

How to store: Moisture and odors are absorbed easily by fresh dates; therefore, they should be tightly covered and stored at a cool temperature between 32° and 40°. Shelf life of packaged dates is four to six months. An opened package of dates will keep only for two months.

How to prepare: Use pitted dates when a recipe calls for a measured amount of dates. Using a small paring knife, cut a lengthwise slit in the date, rolling out the pit with the tip of the knife. For those recipes which require dates to be diced or cubed, cut the fruit on a wooden cutting board with a knife or kitchen shears frequently dipped in cold water. Avoid mincing dates or chopping in fine pieces as they will bind together in a sticky mass.

How to use: Eat dates right from the package as a delicious confection; or, pit, cut up, and toss into a breakfast cereal, fruit salad, or fruit cup. Serve dates in malted milk shakes or ice cream sodas, or sprinkle some of them over a pudding.

Use packaged dates in baked goods, candies, and to make mouth-watering desserts. Bake snipped or chopped dates in muffins, cookies, pies, and cakes. Stuff dates with such delectable delights as fondants, maraschino-flavored marzipan, or a chopped hazelnut, honey, and sugar mixture. For dessert, roll stuffed dates in crushed macaroon or cereal crumbs, fry quickly in deep fat, and serve with a creamy vanilla sauce.

The wholesome fruit, when served with milk, is believed to be a nearly perfect meal. Athletes rely on sweet dates as a source of quick energy.

The stately date palm has many uses besides bearing fruit. In tropical climates the palm leaves are woven into roofs, walls, and baskets, and the fibrous tree bark is twisted into a type of rope. The date pits may be roasted and made into a beverage brewed like coffee, or the mashed pulp made into wine. The Arabs still use dates as feed for livestock by mashing the pitted pulps into cakes. (See also *Fruit*.)

Sweet Potato-Date Puffs

Golden sweet potatoes and date bits form honey-glazed potato balls atop thick pineapple slices—

  1 17-ounce can sweet potatoes,
        drained
  ¾ cup snipped dates
  6 slices canned pineapple
        • • •
  ¼ cup butter or margarine
  ¼ cup brown sugar
  2 tablespoons honey

Mash sweet potatoes; stir in ¼ *cup* of the dates. Shape into six balls. Drain pineapple, reserving 2 tablespoons syrup. Melt butter or margarine in medium skillet; stir in brown sugar, honey, reserved pineapple syrup, and the remaining dates. Heat till sugar is dissolved.

Place 6 slices pineapple into syrup in skillet; top each with a potato ball. Cover; simmer over low heat for 10 to 12 minutes, spooning pineapple syrup over potatoes several times during cooking. Makes 6 servings.

Ginger-Date Triangles

Easy party sandwiches of canned date-nut roll sliced and spread with ginger-flavored filling—

  1 3-ounce package cream cheese,
        softened
  1 tablespoon milk
  1 tablespoon finely snipped
        candied ginger
        • • •
  1 8-ounce can date-nut roll

Blend together cheese and milk; stir in candied ginger. Slice date-nut roll into slices about ⅜ inch thick. Spread half the slices with cream cheese mixture. Top with remaining date-nut slices. Cut each sandwich in quarters. Chill thoroughly. Makes about 20 triangles.

Hot braided coffee cake

Build a good cook's reputation with this→ date Braided Coffee Cake. Rich date filling and nut topper makes it a special feast.

Stuffed Date Drops

Dates stuffed with nuts and dropped in cookie dough become golden delights topped with icing—

½ pound (about 39) pitted dates
  About 39 pecan or walnut halves
¼ cup shortening
¾ cup brown sugar
1 egg
½ cup dairy sour cream
1¼ cups sifted all-purpose flour
½ teaspoon baking powder
½ teaspoon baking soda
¼ teaspoon salt

· · ·

6 tablespoons butter
2 cups sifted confectioners'
  sugar
¼ teaspoon vanilla
  Hot water

Stuff pitted dates with walnuts or pecan halves. Cream shortening and brown sugar till light and fluffy; beat in egg. Stir in dairy sour cream. Sift all-purpose flour, baking powder, baking soda, and salt; add to creamed mixture. Stir in stuffed dates. Drop onto greased cookie sheet, using one date for each cookie. Bake at 400° for 6 to 8 minutes. Remove immediately; cool. Spread creamy icing over each date drop.

Dates combine with banana, pineapple, and nuts to make a glamorous freeze-ahead salad. Date Soufflé Salads are frozen in paper cups.

To make icing, lightly brown butter in a saucepan. Remove from heat and cool. Gradually beat in confectioners' sugar and vanilla. Slowly add hot water till of spreading consistency (about 2 tablespoons). If necessary, add hot water to thin. Makes about 3 dozen.

Stuffed Dates

A mouth-watering candy treat of dates and nuts—

3 tablespoons butter, softened
3 tablespoons light corn syrup
½ teaspoon shredded orange peel
½ teaspoon vanilla
¼ teaspoon salt
2⅓ cups sifted confectioners'
  sugar

· · ·

  Walnut halves
48 pitted dates

Cream butter; blend in corn syrup, shredded orange peel, vanilla, and salt. Add confectioners' sugar all at once; mix in, first with spoon, then by kneading with hands. Place mixture on board; knead till smooth. Wrap in foil; chill 24 hours. Wrap each nut about ½ teaspoon candy and stuff into date. Makes 48.

Date Soufflé Salads

1 8-ounce package cream cheese,
  softened
¼ cup maple syrup
1 tablespoon lemon juice
1 medium banana, mashed (½ cup)
1 8¾-ounce can crushed
  pineapple, drained
½ cup finely chopped dates
½ cup chopped pecans
1 cup whipping cream

Cream the cheese; beat in maple syrup, lemon juice, and mashed banana. Stir in crushed pineapple, chopped dates, and pecans. Whip cream; fold in. Line 6 to 8 muffin cups with paper bake cups; fill with salad. Freeze till firm. Remove bake cups. If desired, arrange on pineapple and greens; top with maraschino cherry. Let salads stand 15 minutes at room temperature before serving. Makes 6 to 8 servings.

Date Chiffon Pie studded with snipped dates offers an unusual prepare-ahead dessert. The magnificent filling is turned into a cooled cheese pastry for double flavor eating.

Date Chiffon Pie

  1 cup sifted all-purpose flour
  ½ teaspoon salt
  ⅓ cup shortening
  ½ cup shredded sharp process
      American cheese
  3 tablespoons cold water

     • • •

  1 envelope unflavored
      gelatin (1 tablespoon)
  ¼ cup sugar
  2 egg yolks
  ½ cup orange juice
  ⅓ cup lemon juice
  ½ cup light cream
  2 egg whites
  ¼ cup sugar
  1½ cups snipped dates

Prepare cheese pastry by sifting together flour and salt. Cut in ⅓ cup shortening. Add shredded sharp process American cheese; toss lightly. Gradually sprinkle cold water over mixture, tossing with fork till moistened. Roll out on floured surface to ⅛ inch. Fit into 8-inch pie plate, being careful not to stretch the pastry; crimp edges. Prick crust with a fork. Bake at 450° for 8 to 10 minutes.

In a saucepan mix the gelatin and ¼ cup sugar. Beat together the egg yolks and fruit juices; stir into gelatin mixture. Cook and stir over medium heat just till mixture comes to boiling and is slightly thickened. Cool. Stir in cream; chill till slightly thickened. Beat egg whites with dash salt till soft peaks form. Add ¼ cup sugar gradually; beat till stiff peaks form. Fold in gelatin mixture, then dates. Turn into cooled pastry. Chill firm.

Date Cake

½ pound pitted dates, coarsely
    chopped (1½ cups)
½ cup shortening
1 cup sugar
1 teaspoon vanilla
1 egg
1½ cups sifted all-purpose flour
1 teaspoon baking soda
½ cup chopped walnuts

Combine chopped dates with 1 cup boiling water; cool to room temperature. Cream shortening and sugar till light. Add vanilla and egg; beat well. Sift flour, baking soda, and ¼ teaspoon salt together; add to creamed mixture alternately with date mixture, beating after each addition. Stir in chopped walnuts. Bake in greased and lightly floured 13x9x2-inch baking pan at 350° about 25 to 30 minutes. If desired, serve with a dollop of whipped cream.

Easy Date Crumble Torte

1 14-ounce package date bar mix
½ cup chopped walnuts
2 tablespoons melted butter
    or margarine
1 cup frozen whipped dessert
    topping, thawed

Combine the crumb portion of the date bar mix and chopped walnuts; stir in melted butter or margarine, mixing well. Spread in 13x9x2-inch baking pan. Bake at 400° for 10 minutes. Break up with a fork, cool and crumble.

    Prepare date filling according to package directions; cool. Place *half* the crumb mixture in bottom of 10x6x1¾-inch baking dish. Cover with ½ cup thawed whipped dessert topping, then with date mixture. Repeat crumb and whipped topping layers. Chill several hours or overnight. Top each serving with a walnut half, if desired. Makes 8 servings.

A fast dessert idea

← Make Easy Date Crumble Torte using a package date bar mix and frozen dessert topping. Garnish with whole walnuts.

Braided Coffee Cake

1 package active dry yeast
4 to 4¼ cups sifted all-purpose
    flour
1¼ cups milk
½ cup butter or margarine
½ cup granulated sugar
1 egg
    · · ·
1½ cups snipped dates
½ cup brown sugar
½ cup chopped walnuts
2 tablespoons lemon juice
1 egg yolk
2 tablespoons milk
    · · ·
⅓ cup all-purpose flour
¼ cup butter or margarine
2 tablespoons granulated sugar
½ teaspoon ground cinnamon

In large bowl combine yeast and 2½ *cups* flour. Heat together 1¼ cups milk, ½ cup butter, ½ cup granulated sugar, and 1 teaspoon salt till warm, stirring to melt butter. Add to dry mixture in bowl; add egg. Beat at low speed with electric mixer for ½ minute, scraping sides of bowl. Beat 3 minutes at high speed. By hand, stir in enough remaining 1½ to 1¾ cups flour to make moderately stiff dough. Cover and refrigerate at least 2 hours or overnight.

    Divide dough in half. On lightly floured surface, roll each half to 14x8-inch rectangle. Place rectangles on greased baking sheets. Spread half the Date Filling lengthwise down center third of each rectangle. Cut 12 slits, about 1 inch apart, in dough along each side of filling. Fold strips at an angle across filling, alternating from side to side. Cover; let rise till double, about 1 hour. Combine egg yolk and 2 tablespoons milk. Brush dough with egg mixture using a pastry brush. Sprinkle half the Topping on top of each coffee cake. Bake at 350° for 30 to 35 minutes. Makes 2 coffee cakes.

    Date Filling: In a saucepan combine dates, brown sugar, 1 cup water, walnuts, and lemon juice. Bring to boil over medium heat, stirring constantly. Continue boiling gently, stirring occasionally, till mixture is thick enough to spread, about 8 minutes. Cool.

    Topping: Combine ⅓ cup flour, ¼ cup butter or margarine, 2 tablespoons sugar, and ground cinnamon; mix well.

DAUBE *(dōb)* — A French stew of braised meat, vegetables, herbs and seasonings, and sometimes red wine. Different regions in France have specialty daubes, such as *Daube a l'Avignonnaise,* which is lamb cubes cooked in red wine with onions and bacon, and *Daube a la Provencale,* which is a beef stew containing olives, mushrooms, onions, and tomatoes.

Deep, covered earthenware, a heavy braising pot, or Dutch oven is used to cook the stew slowly on top of the range or in the oven. The procedure resembles braising. The stew is better when made a day in advance because the flavors develop more and may be served hot or cold.

DECAFFEINATED COFFEE *(dē kaf′ uh nāt′ uhd, - kaf′ ē uh -)* — Regular, instant, or freeze-dried coffee from which almost all caffein has been extracted. Decaffeinated coffee was developed in the early 1920s to provide a coffee beverage for those people who are affected by caffeine present in regular coffee. Although the caffeine is removed from the coffee before roasting the coffee beans, manufacturers have developed special processing techniques so that the desired coffee flavor is maintained. Decaffeinated coffee is available in several forms for brewing in a coffeemaker or preparing instantly in the cup with the addition of water. (See also *Coffee.*)

DECANT *(di kant′)* — The process of gently pouring red wine from its bottle into another container, leaving the sediment behind. (White wines do not collect a heavy sediment so decanting is not necessary for them.) Traditionally, a lighted candle was placed behind the bottle so that when the wine was poured out, the movement of the sediment could be observed.

Sometimes the wine is poured through a cloth to screen out the sediment, cork particles, and other impurities. Decanting should be completed at least an hour before the wine is to be served.

DECANTER — A container made of ceramic, glass, plastic, or metal in which wines, liquors, and liqueurs may be kept. These decorative vessels became popular because it was believed that the label exposing the manufacturer's or shipper's name was commercial and not a gracious way to serve guests. Most fine decanters are made of crystal and topped with an elaborate stopper. By custom, shapes vary according to use: short, squatty ones with long necks for port or sherry, sturdy taller ones for whiskies, and dainty ones for liqueurs. (See also *Wines* and *Spirits.*)

DECORETTE — This is the overall term for the tiny candies used to garnish cakes and cookies, such as chocolate shot, silver and gold dragees, and varicolored dots, shreds, and assorted shapes.

DEEP-DISH PIE — A one-crust pie (top crust only) with sliced, diced, or whole fruit filling. The sweetened, spiced fruit is placed in a deep pie pan, shallow baking pan, or individual dishes and then covered with pastry. To prevent boiling over during baking, a custard cup or small inverted cup is sometimes placed in the center to draw up some of the juices. Slashes should be made in the pastry to allow for steam to escape during baking.

In some recipes, the pie is baked in a 450° oven for 10 to 15 minutes, then reduced to 350° so both fruit and crust will bake. The result is a cross between a

The old "as American as apple pie" slogan takes on special note with this Deep-Dish Apple Pie served with Custard Sauce.

"spoon dessert" and a regular pie. A deep-dish pie is somewhat like a fruit cobbler made with a pastry rather than biscuit crust. (See also *Pie*.)

Custard-Sauced Deep-Dish Apple Pie

      8 large tart apples, peeled,
          cored, and sliced (8 cups)
    ¾ to 1 cup sugar
      1 teaspoon ground nutmeg
      1 tablespooon butter or margarine
          Plain pastry for 1-crust
            9-inch pie (See *Pastry*)
      1 cup light cream
      2 slightly beaten egg yolks
    ¼ cup sugar

Place apples in 9x9x2-inch baking dish. Combine sugar and nutmeg; sprinkle atop apples. Dot with butter. Prepare pastry; roll into a 10-inch square ⅛ inch thick. Place over filling, cutting slits for escape of steam. Crimp to edges of dish. Bake at 425° for 40 minutes.

Serve with *Custard Sauce:* Combine cream, egg yolks, and sugar in top of double boiler. Cook over hot water, stirring constantly, till mixture coats a metal spoon.

Deep-Dish Orange-Peach Pie

    ¾ cup sugar
      3 tablespoons all-purpose flour
      1 teaspoon grated orange peel
          Dash ground nutmeg
      2 cups orange sections, cut up
      1 29-ounce can sliced peaches,
            drained
      2 tablespoons butter or margarine
          Plain pastry for 1-crust 9-inch
            pie (See *Pastry*)

Combine sugar, flour, orange peel, and nutmeg. Mix with orange sections and canned peaches. Turn into 8x8x2-inch baking dish. Dot with butter or margarine.

Prepare pastry. Roll into a square, ⅛ inch thick; cut in 9-inch square. Place atop orange-peach filling, cutting slits for escape of steam. Crimp pastry to edges of baking dish. Bake at 400° about 40 minutes. Serve warm.

DEEP-FAT FRY—A cookery method in which food is completely immersed in hot fat.

One of the oldest recorded cookery methods, deep-fat frying in olive oil was used by ancient Romans. Oriental tempura dishes were also early successful beginnings of the deep-fat frying technique.

The eating quality of the food is largely dependent on the way the food is readied for frying, the type of fat used, and the frying temperature of the fat. A properly cooked deep-fat fried food has a crisp outside and a moist, tender interior. Less fat is absorbed by the product than when cooking in a smaller amount of fat because deep-fat frying is faster.

A longer cooking period and larger pieces increase the fat absorption, so precooking is sometimes necessary. Cut food into small pieces (two to three inches in diameter) and fry only a few at a time so fat absorption will not be lowered and excessive bubbling will be avoided. The pieces should be somewhat uniform in size so they will fry evenly and brown nicely at the same time. Be sure to dry moist foods, such as potatoes, with paper toweling before frying, to minimize spattering.

Many kinds of foods are suited to deep frying. These include vegetables, such as potatoes, eggplant, cauliflower, squash, or onion rings; any kind of croquettes; meats and fish, such as veal, chicken, fish, or shrimp; doughnuts and crullers; fruits; and hearty and sweet fritters.

Most foods prepared for frying are coated to give them a pleasing, crunchy texture. Fine crumbs or crushed cereals adhere well to the surface during cooking. Before rolling the food in crumbs, dip in milk and egg batter. When food pieces are dipped in egg before the crumbs, let excess egg drip off, then crumb the pieces evenly. Drain batter-dipped foods on a wire cake rack before frying.

Croquettes are made by combining meats with vegetables and then coating with eggs and crumbs and fried. Excess crumbs floating in the fat will lower the temperature so make sure crumbs adhere.

Fritters are made by mixing the basic food, such as corn kernels or fruit pieces, right into a batter which is dropped into the pot from a spoon.

Dip shrimp butterflies in a curried flour mixture and then into bubbling hot fat till golden brown. Keep controlled frying temperature by frying a few shrimp at a time and removing loose particles in the fat with a slotted spoon. Drain shrimp on paper toweling. Foods prepared in this manner are sometimes called French-fried.

Remove French-Fried Butterfly Shrimp from absorbent paper to heated platter. Serve at once. Eat the crisp shrimp by picking up by the tail and biting into the meat part of shrimp. For hors d'oeuvres, serve with chutney and lemon wedges. For a main course, serve with chili or tartar sauce.

Fats for deep-fat frying

Fats with a high smoking point such as salad oils and all-purpose shortenings are best for deep-fat frying. Do not use olive oil, butter, or margarine. At high temperatures they give off irritating aromas and fumes.

Maintain a constant frying temperature for uniform, evenly browned food. Use tongs or a long-handled fork to remove food and place on absorbent paper toweling. Cool, strain, and refrigerate oil for future frying use. If oil has absorbed a strong flavor, such as fish, reuse it again for future frying use. (See also *Fry.*)

French-Fried Butterfly Shrimp

Peel shells from 2 pounds large raw shrimp, leaving tails. Slit shrimp along back; remove sand vein, flatten shrimp. Make cut in center back; pull tail through. Pat shrimp dry. Combine 1 cup sifted all-purpose flour, ½ teaspoon sugar, ½ teaspoon salt, and dash curry powder; add 1 egg, 1 cup water, and 2 tablespoons salad oil; beat well. Dip shrimp in batter; fry in deep hot fat (375°) till brown. Remove cooked shrimp to paper toweling to drain; serve at once. Makes 4 to 6 servings.

DEEP-FAT FRYER—A deep, heavy, three- to four-quart kettle used to fry foods in deep fat. It may be a deep saucepan, Dutch oven, electric skillet, or saucepan fitted with a long-handled wire basket and hooks to catch on pan edge, keeping basket off the bottom. A deep-fat thermometer, clipped to pan side, indicates temperature.

There is a portable electric deep-fat fryer with thermostatic temperature regulator to be used on counter or table. Besides frying, it's used for stewing, braising, pot roasting, soup making, or corn-popping. Use it to blanch vegetables for home freezing or to steam puddings, to stew dried fruits, to make applesauce, or to heat punch or chocolate drink.

Take good care of the deep-fat fryer by cleaning thoroughly after every use. Empty out fat, wipe inside with paper toweling, then wash it with hot sudsy water. Scrub out stains. Rinse thoroughly with clear water; dry well. Follow manufacturers' directions for cleaning and care instructions. (See also *Equipment*.)

DEER—A type of wild game whose edible flesh is called venison. The age of the animal is important to the meat flavor and texture. A fawn is not more than six months old and a stag is five years or older. The hunting season with regard to age and sex of deer and limit is state regulated.

Fresh deer should be hung in a cool place to age from 5 days to a month depending on age and condition of the animal. Deer cuts are the same as for beef and can be cut by a butcher. Also similar to beef cuts as far as tenderness is concerned, deer can be cooked like any other meat. Recipe for deer, moose, and elk are interchangeable. (See also *Venison*.)

DEGLAZE—Adding liquid to a roasting pan after meat and fat have been removed to loosen adhering meat bits. Wine, soup stock, or other liquid is used to remove the succulent browned particles so that they can add flavor to a gravy or sauce.

DEHYDRATION *(dē hī drā' shun)*—Removal of water from fruits and vegetables for preservation purposes.

A berry or fruit shriveled by the sun was probably man's first encounter with dehydrated food. People dried food thousands of years ago—Stone Age people dried legumes and Persians dried figs. Greeks and Romans used dried peas, and the early American Indian settlers dried corn.

Dehydration may be carried out in three separate ways. 1. Sun-drying is done with fruits picked at the peak of ripeness, spread on trays, and sunned for a limited time. They are moved to a shady place to cure, where the minute amount of moisture left spreads throughout the piece. 2. Dehydration is also carried out by drying food in mechanically circulated air currents, some heated then cooled; in a variety of machines; and drying chambers. Dried fruits, dried beans, and dried corn products are some of the most common dehydrated goods. 3. A recently introduced

dehydration process, known as freeze-drying, concerns the removal of water from frozen food in a vacuum. Familiar examples include camping supplies, dry soup mixes containing vegetable, and instant coffee crystals. (See also *Dried Fruit*.)

DELICIOUS APPLE—An apple discovered by Jesse Hiatt of Peru, Iowa, in 1872. Named the *Hawkeye*, it was purchased by Stark Brothers in 1895 and introduced commercially as *Delicious*. In 1900, a man named Mullins discovered a golden-yellow apple in his West Virginia orchard. Purchased also by the Stark Brothers in 1916, it was named the *Golden Delicious*. Now Delicious apples lead the national apple production with Washington state the top commercial grower of this variety.

Both varieties are recognized by the five points on the bottom. The Red Delicious apple with thick red strips against a yellow background and a pleasant subacid taste is best used for salads and desserts.

The popular Golden Delicious is more firm and tart than the Red Delicious. It can be used for pies, sauces, and baking, but remember that it is sweeter than most cooking apples so little sugar is needed. It does not brown when cut so is excellent for fruit salads. (See also *Apple*.)

DEMERARA *(de' muh ruh)*—A region in Guiana, South America, where dark, heavy, and high-proof rum is distilled, and where a special sugar is refined. (See *Rum, Sugar* for additional information.)

DEMI-GLAZE—A French term for a brown sauce simmered slowly to reduce its volume and concentrate its flavor. Flavored with wine, it is used as a base in making other sauces. (See also *Sauce*.)

DEMI-SEC—A French term for a sweet champagne or wine which is drier than sweet *doux* but sweeter than *sec* which is dry but not as dry as brut. (See also *Champagne*.)

DEMI-SEL CHEESE—A soft, creamy, lightly salted cream cheese made in Normandy, France. The fragile cheese is consumed where it is made because it is so highly perishable. (See also *Cream Cheese*.)

This delightful entertaining idea gives just reason to bring out tiny demitasse cup collections. Frosted petits fours served with the double-strength Demitasse gives miniature elegance to special occasions.

DEMITASSE *(dem' i tas', täs')* — 1. A dark, fragrant coffee usually served after dinner. 2. The small half-size cup used for serving the dark coffee. Demi means half and tasse means cup. Demitasse was traditionally served black, but cream and sugar are now acceptable additions.

The stronger brew is made by reducing the amount of water used for each standard measuring cup. Enhance the after-dinner coffee by pouring it from a handsome silver pot. Offer elegant toppings such as crushed cinnamon or peppermint candies, shredded orange peel, and fat curls of sweet baking chocolate in separate little individual bowls. Offer whipped cream and make demitasse a special dessert. Add flavor and a bit of color to the tiny drink with a teaspoon of lemon or orange juice and a twist of peel.

Demitasse may be served at cocktail time for those not wishing alcoholic drinks. However, hot demitasse mixes well with brandies and liqueurs, such as white crème de menthe, curacao, kummel, anisette, and Cointreau. (See also *Coffee*.)

Demitasse

Brew coffee as usual but use only ½ cup water, instead of usual ¾ cup, for each 2 level measuring tablespoons of coffee. (A standard coffee measure holds 2 level measuring tablespoons.)

DENVER SANDWICH — A sandwich made of eggs scrambled with ham, chopped onions, and green peppers. Also called the Western Sandwich, it was invented by the pioneers. As eggs were being transported over long, hot trails, they would start to decompose and become tainted. The alert pioneer woman would salvage the eggs and kill the strong flavor with onions, bacon fat, and any available seasonings on hand. The mixture was then served as a sandwich filling on bread.

A sophisticated version of the Denver sandwich might be an egg omelet combined with sautéed ham, onion, and green pepper. Sometimes bacon bits are used instead of ham, and the bread may or may not be toasted. (See also *Sandwich*.)

Dad's Denvers

A quick snack sandwich using canned ham, topped with eggs and broiled for hearty goodness—

Split and toast 6 hamburger buns. Spread lower half of buns with one 4½-ounce can deviled ham. Combine 4 eggs, ¼ cup milk, and dash pepper. Beat slightly for gold-and-white effect, thoroughly for all-yellow effect. Add ¼ cup chopped green onion; mix well.

Heat 2 tablespoons butter or bacon drippings in skillet till just hot enough to make water drop sizzle. Pour in beaten egg mixture. Reduce heat and cook, lifting and folding occasionally, till eggs are set, but still moist. Pile cooked eggs atop deviled ham.

Place sandwiches on baking sheet; broil about 4 inches from heat 3 to 4 minutes. Top *each* sandwich with 1 thin tomato slice and then 1 slice sharp process American cheese. Broil just till cheese melts. Cover hot sandwiches with bun tops. Makes 6 servings.

Denver Sandwich

¼ cup finely chopped onion
2 tablespoons finely chopped green pepper
1 tablespoon butter or margarine
4 slightly beaten eggs
½ cup finely chopped fully cooked ham
¼ cup milk
1 tablespoon chopped canned pimiento
4 buns, split, buttered, and toasted, *or* 8 slices bread, buttered and toasted, if desired

In skillet cook onion and green pepper in butter till tender. Combine eggs, ham, milk, pimiento, dash salt, and dash pepper. Pour into skillet with onion mixture. Cook over low heat, lifting and folding occasionally, just until set. Spoon mixture between bun halves or between bread or toast slices. Makes 4 servings.

Delicious Dad's Denvers become special treats to all family members. Eggs scrambled with deviled ham and onions sport a tomato and melted cheese topper. Serve with soup or salad.

DESSERT

A guide to a delicious final course—either quick and simple or elegant and impressive.

Traditionally, the dessert is the final course served at a noonday or evening meal, but it need not be an afterthought. You can make it the course to remember.

The name is derived from the French word *desservir* meaning "to clear the table," for at one time the dessert was served after everything had been removed from the table, including the tablecloth. Later, it was served before removing the tablecloth and was accompanied by a small cup of coffee, a glass of brandy, and several cigarettes placed on a small silver tray to the right of each dinner guest.

During the nineteenth century, elaborate meals staged by the French included a spectacular array of fresh fruit arranged in decorative baskets and used as a part of the table decoration. In addition, an assortment of mouth-watering sweets surrounded the fruit baskets. Near the close of the meal, cheese was passed to accompany the wine and this was followed by a dessert of fresh fruit and sweets.

Today, national custom dictates to a large degree the pattern followed in serving dessert. In some European countries, a cheese course still precedes the sweet, which in turn is followed with fresh fruit. The English, however, prefer to serve cheese after the sweet. The traditional American dessert offers any of these— cheese, fruit, or sweet—singly or in combination, as typified by the favorite fresh apple pie with cheese wedge.

A spectacular ending

←Strawberry Meringue Cake tempts guests for second helpings. Meringue-topped cake mix sports strawberries and whipped cream.

Some desserts are linked traditionally to special celebrations or holidays. Pumpkin pie tops off the bountiful Thanksgiving Day feast, while fruitcake adds a festive air to the Christmas holiday. Cake, decorated or plain, is popular fare for birthdays, weddings, and anniversaries. In addition, fresh fruit pies and homemade ice cream mark summertime socials.

The dessert course serves many functions, one of them being the hostess's opportunity to leave a favorable impression with her dinner guests. If well planned, the dessert completes an enjoyable, yet satisfying meal. It should not dominate the food which precedes it; neither should it be lost or ignored. If the meal is hearty, a light dessert is in order; if the meal is light, a more filling dessert provides needed contrast. Thus, dessert may vary from a simple fruit cup to a dramatic flaming fruit combination served in a chafing dish.

Some desserts are rich in vitamins, minerals, and/or calories. Among the more nutritious meal-endings are those prepared with fruit, milk, and eggs. The well-planned menu takes advantage of the final course to add important nutrients to the meal—not just calories. However, in too many cases, dessert is synonymous with calories. Yet, the weight-conscious individual need not despair. Low-calorie ingredients make possible a wide variety of desserts. A further control of calories is possible with the wise selection of dessert garnishes, such as fresh fruit slices, flavored-gelatin cutouts, shredded citrus peel, ground cinnamon, ground nutmeg, or low-calorie dessert toppings.

The abundance of convenience dessert items on the market, both partially prepared and ready-to-eat, attest to the popularity of dessert in the American home.

Many homemakers prefer to devote most of the meal preparation time to the main dish; thus, convenience dessert mixes not only simplify meal preparation, but also are a boon to the cook who wishes to add variety to her repertoire of desserts.

Mixes, such as cake, cookie, frosting, piecrust, custard, dessert topping, and pudding, make possible a wide variety of desserts which can be prepared on short notice. Variations of commercial mixes are used to prepare a grand assortment of delicious desserts which often mask their simplicity. In addition, ready-to-eat canned puddings and frozen cakes, pies, and cheesecakes eliminate all preparation.

Types of desserts

The classification of desserts into types is at best overlapping. Some desserts are frozen or chilled, while others are baked, steamed, broiled, or fried. The texture may be rich and creamy, soft and delicate, light and foamy, or crisp and chewy. Flavor varies from very sweet to slightly tart. Despite these differences, certain characteristics are apparent among many desserts due to the similarity of ingredients and methods of mixing used in preparation.

Fruit desserts: Many desserts are made with fruit, fruit-flavored ingredients, or are served with fruit. However, fruit is an excellent dessert served alone and provides a simple, yet refreshing ending for lunch or dinner. In addition, it is one of the most nutritious desserts since it is relatively high in many of the essential vitamins and minerals and low in calories.

Some of the more popular desserts are a mixture of several fruits. Fruit ambrosia, in which coconut is tossed with assorted fruits, makes an attractive dessert. Likewise, compotes, made by cooking fruits in a sugary syrup, are delicious. Fruit soups may be served either as an appetizer or as a dessert. Although fruit fritters are most often served with the main course in American homes, they are popular served as the dessert course in Europe and many other sections of the world.

Fruits such as apples and rhubarb may be cooked in water till tender and then sweetened to make a dessert sauce. Other fruit sauces are served over ice cream or cake and are made by thickening the fruit syrup with a little cornstarch. The whole fruit is then stirred into the thickened liquid for an attractive sauce.

Fruit is often baked to prepare such favorites as apple dumplings, apple crisp, and apple betty. The combination of fruit with pastry is excellent as evidenced by the popularity of fruit pies, cobblers, tarts, turnovers, and shortcakes.

The different forms of fruit available—fresh, canned, frozen, and dried—as well as the wide variety of fruits make fruit desserts possible year-round. Fruit lends itself to many methods of preparation including baking, stewing, broiling, and frying. Thus, fruit may be served as simply as "an apple a day," or as elegantly as flaming Cherries Jubilee.

Cherry Melange

An elegant dessert for an evening buffet—

> 1 14½-ounce can pitted dark sweet cherries, drained and halved *or* 2 cups fresh dark sweet cherries, pitted and halved
> 1 cup fresh strawberries, sliced
> 1 cup cantaloupe balls (about ⅓ of a cantaloupe)
> 1 13½-ounce can frozen pineapple chunks, thawed and drained
> . . .
> ½ cup orange marmalade
> ¼ cup hot water
> 1 teaspoon snipped candied ginger
> 1 medium-large banana, sliced
> Fresh mint

Chill dark sweet cherries, sliced strawberries, and cantaloupe balls. Layer chilled fruits and drained pineapple chunks in compote, glass bowl, or 8 sherbet glasses. Combine orange marmalade, hot water, and candied ginger. Drizzle mixture over fruit. Chill.

When ready to serve, arrange banana slices atop fruit. (To prevent banana slices from darkening, dip in lemon juice or ascorbic acid color keeper.) Garnish fruit with sprigs of fresh mint. Makes 8 servings.

Strawberry Cream

  1 3-ounce package cream cheese,
    softened
  2 tablespoons sugar
  1 cup whipping cream
    Fresh whole strawberries,
    hulled

In small mixing bowl combine cheese, sugar, dash salt, and *2 tablespoons* of the whipping cream; beat till fluffy. Whip remaining cream; carefully fold cream into cheese mixture. Spoon over berries. Makes 1¾ cups sauce.

Custard desserts: Custard provides a simple, yet versatile dessert. Often flavored with vanilla, custard is delicious served alone or topped with fruit. A delicate custard sauce is a good substitute for cream, whipped cream, or ice cream served over fruit pies, steamed puddings, or cakes. A flavorful custard dessert—crème brûlée—features stirred custard sprinkled with brown sugar; just before serving, it is placed under the broiler to caramelize the sugar. Baked custard is an equally satisfying and nutritious dessert accompanied with fruit or baked in a pastry shell.

Pumpkin Crème Brûlée

  1 cup canned pumpkin
  3 slightly beaten eggs
  ½ cup granulated sugar
  ½ teaspoon grated orange peel
  ½ teaspoon ground cinnamon
  ¼ teaspoon ground allspice
  1 14-ounce can evaporated milk
    (1⅔ cups)
  ¼ cup brown sugar

Combine first 6 ingredients; slowly stir in milk. Fill six 5-ounce custard cups; set in shallow baking pan on oven rack. Pour hot water into pan 1 inch deep. Bake at 325° till knife inserted halfway between center and edge comes out clean, 50 to 55 minutes. Chill.

Sift brown sugar over custards. Set in shallow baking pan of ice cubes and cold water. Broil 5 inches from heat till bubbly crust forms, about 5 minutes. Chill. Serves 6.

Pudding desserts: Puddings are thickened with cornstarch, tapioca, rice, bread, or other cereal. Fruit, chocolate, caramel, and nuts are often added for variety. Some puddings are baked in the oven; others are stirred in a saucepan during cooking.

Puddings thickened with cornstarch have a smooth and creamy texture and many be served warm or chilled. In addition, they may be used as fillings for cakes, pies, cream puffs, and other desserts.

Unlike other types of puddings, steamed puddings have a cakelike texture. Usually served with a hard sauce or fruit sauce, they often contain dried, canned, or fresh fruit. Delicious served warm, steamed puddings are a favorite holiday dessert.

Blueberry Steamed Pudding

  ½ cup butter or margarine
  1 cup sugar
  2 eggs
  ½ teaspoon vanilla
  2 cups sifted all-purpose flour
  3 teaspoons baking powder
  ½ teaspoon salt
  ½ teaspoon ground cinnamon
  ¾ cup milk
  2 tablespoons lemon juice
  2½ cups fresh blueberries
    Blueberry Sauce

Cream butter or margarine and sugar. Add eggs and vanilla; mix well. Sift together flour, baking powder, salt, and cinnamon. Add alternately with milk to creamed mixture, beating well after each addition. Stir in lemon juice. Fold in *1½ cups* of the blueberries.

Pour into well-greased and floured 5½-cup mold. Cover with foil; tie with string. Place on rack in deep kettle. Add boiling water, 1 inch deep. Cover; steam 2 hours, adding water, if needed. Cool 20 minutes; unmold. Slice, if desired; serve warm with sauce. Serves 8.

Blueberry Sauce: Mix ½ cup sugar, 1 tablespoon cornstarch, ⅛ teaspoon ground nutmeg, and dash salt. Stir in ½ cup boiling water. Cook and stir till bubbly; cook and stir 2 minutes more. Stir in remaining 1 cup blueberries. Return to boiling; cook mixture just till berries begin to pop. Remove from heat; stir in 1 tablespoon lemon juice. Makes 1½ cups.

Cookie desserts: Cookies provide a light dessert for lunch and are ideal for boxed lunches. Prepared ahead, they can be stored in a cookie jar or frozen until needed. For a more filling dessert, they are often served with fruit or ice cream.

Cookies may also be used in preparing refrigerated or baked desserts. They add flavor and crunch when crushed to make a crumb crust for pies. Likewise, crushed gingersnaps or macaroons make a flavorful garnish sprinkled over desserts.

Cherry Cookie Crisp

    1 16-ounce can pitted tart red
        cherries (water pack)
    1 teaspoon lemon juice
      Few drops red food coloring
    ⅓ cup sugar
    ½ teaspoon ground cinnamon
    1½ cups vanilla wafer crumbs
    ⅓ cup butter or margarine, melted

Drain tart red cherries, reserving 2 tablespoons juice. Mix cherries, reserved juice, lemon juice, and few drops red food coloring. Pour into 10x 6x1¾-inch baking dish. Sprinkle mixture of sugar and cinnamon atop dessert. Combine vanilla wafer crumbs and melted butter or margarine; pat over cherries. Bake at 400° for 25 minutes. Serve dessert warm. Serves 6.

Apricot-Scotch Cobbler

    1 21-ounce can apricot pie
        filling*
    1 roll refrigerated butterscotch-
        nut cookie dough, sliced ¼
        inch thick
    1 teaspoon sugar
      Dash ground cinnamon

Heat pie filling; pour into 8-inch pie plate. Slightly overlap cookie slices atop filling around edge of pie plate. (Bake any remaining cookies separately for snacks.) Sprinkle cookies on filling with mixture of sugar and cinnamon. Bake at 350° till cookies are done, about 25 minutes. Serve warm or cold; top with ice cream, if desired. Makes 5 servings.

*Substitute any flavor pie filling as desired.

Cake desserts: Glamorous or plain, cake is an all-time dessert favorite. Texture varies from the light and airy chiffons to the fruit-laden holiday cakes. Made in assorted sizes, shapes, and flavors, cake is often accompanied with fruit or ice cream.

Cake makes possible countless desserts, such as baked Alaskas, tortes, upside-down cakes, and jelly rolls. Cake is also popular layered with a cream filling.

Strawberry-Meringue Cake

    1 package 2-layer-size yellow
        cake mix
    1 cup orange juice
    4 egg yolks
    1 teaspoon grated orange peel
        •   •   •
    4 egg whites
    ¼ teaspoon cream of tartar
    1 cup sugar
    1 quart fresh strawberries,
        hulled
    2 cups whipping cream
    ¼ cup sugar

Combine cake mix, orange juice, ⅓ cup water, egg yolks, and orange peel; beat 4 minutes on medium speed of electric mixer.

Pour into 2 greased and waxed paper-lined 9x1½-inch round cake pans. Beat egg whites with cream of tartar to soft peaks; gradually add the 1 cup sugar, beating to stiff peaks. Gently spread meringue evenly over batter. Bake at 350° for 35 to 40 minutes; cool.

With flexible spatulas, carefully remove cake from pans, keeping meringue sides up. Set aside a few berries for garnish; slice remainder.

Whip cream with the ¼ cup sugar. Spread ⅔ of the whipped cream over meringue on bottom cake layer. Arrange sliced berries on whipped cream. Add top layer, meringue side up. Garnish dessert with remaining whipped cream and reserved whole strawberries.

A dessert to remember

Quick and easy Peach-Pecan Mold presents→ an ice cream sundae in a new version. Prepare ahead and assemble just before serving.

Refrigerator desserts: A variety of desserts that require refrigeration before serving. Often they are prepared with flavored or unflavored gelatin combined with a fruit mixture. Chilling the dessert mixture results in the formation of a gel.

Sometimes the mixture is whipped to produce a light and airy texture characteristic of whips, sponges, Bavarian creams, and snows. The addition of beaten egg whites, whipped cream, or whipped evaporated milk further increases the volume of the final dessert product.

Desserts such as cheesecakes and tortes are baked and then chilled before serving. Likewise, parfait and chiffon pies must be refrigerated until they are firm.

Refrigerator desserts are easy to serve since they can be prepared in advance. For added convenience, some may be chilled in individual serving dishes.

Snowflake Pudding

    1 cup sugar
    1½ tablespoons unflavored gelatin
    1¼ cups milk
    1 teaspoon vanilla
    1⅓ cups flaked coconut
    2 cups whipping cream
       Raspberry Sauce

In saucepan combine sugar, gelatin, and ½ teaspoon salt; add milk. Stir over medium heat till gelatin dissolves. Chill till partially set.

Stir in vanilla. Fold in coconut. Whip cream; fold into pudding. Pile into 6½-cup mold; chill till firm, at least 6 hours or overnight. Unmold; serve with Raspberry Sauce. Serves 8.

Raspberry Sauce: Thaw and crush one 10-ounce package frozen raspberries. Combine with 1 tablespoon cornstarch. Add ½ cup currant jelly. Cook, stirring constantly, till thick and bubbly; cook and stir 1 minute more. Strain sauce; cool. Makes 1¼ cups sauce.

Cool and refreshing

←Chilled Cherry Melange or frosty Strawberry Parfaits provide the perfect ending for a summertime luncheon or barbecue.

Frozen desserts: Ice cream, ice milk, and sherbet are favorite desserts served from the freezer. Their popularity is apparent by the wide variety of flavors available in supermarkets and ice cream shops. When prepared at home, they are considered a specialty. Other home-frozen desserts include mousses and parfaits.

Ice cream is a quick and easy dessert topped with fruit or sauce. Moreover, pies, cakes, and other desserts are sometimes served à la mode. Slightly lower in calories, sherbet provides a refreshing dessert at the end of a heavy meal.

Ice cream and sherbet may also be used in preparing baked Alaska. The meringue acts as an insulator to prevent the ice cream from melting during baking.

Strawberry Parfaits

    1 pint fresh strawberries, hulled
    1½ teaspoons unflavored gelatin
    2 tablespoons cold water
    2 cups buttermilk
    ¾ cup sugar
    ½ teaspoon vanilla
    1 to 2 drops red food coloring
          · · ·
    2 egg whites
    ⅓ cup sugar
          · · ·
    1 pint fresh strawberries, hulled

Put 1 pint strawberries through food mill or sieve to make puree. Soften gelatin in cold water; heat over hot water till gelatin dissolves. Combine buttermilk, ¾ cup sugar, strawberry puree, vanilla, food coloring, and gelatin; mix well. Turn into one 6-cup or two 3-cup refrigerator trays; freeze firm. Break into chunks; turn into chilled bowl.

Beat smooth with electric or rotary beater. Beat egg whites till soft peaks form. Gradually add ⅓ cup sugar, beating to stiff peaks.

Fold into strawberry mixture. Return mixture to cold refrigerator tray; freeze firm.

To serve, reserve a few whole strawberries from 1 pint strawberries; slice remaining berries and sweeten to taste. Spoon frozen mixture and sliced berries alternately into parfait glasses. Garnish with reserved whole berries. Serve immediately. Makes 7 or 8 servings.

Peach–Pecan Mold

> 1 quart vanilla ice cream
> 2 teaspoons rum flavoring
> ½ cup chopped pecans
>   Pecan halves
>   Peach Sauce

Stir ice cream to soften. Stir in flavoring and chopped nuts. Arrange a few pecan halves in top of 4½-cup mold. Add ice cream; freeze till firm, about 6 hours. To unmold, invert on serving plate; press hot damp towel around mold to loosen. If desired, garnish with pressurized dessert topping and thawed frozen sliced peaches. Serve with Peach Sauce.

Peach Sauce: In saucepan stir one 12-ounce can peach nectar (1½ cups) into 1 tablespoon cornstarch. Add ¼ cup light corn syrup. Cook and stir till thick and bubbly; cook and stir 2 minutes longer. Stir in 1 tablespoon butter, 1 tablespoon lemon juice, and dash ground mace; cool. Just before serving, add one 12-ounce package frozen peaches, thawed, drained, and coarsely chopped. Makes 6 to 8 servings.

Strawberry Squares

> 1 cup sifted all-purpose flour
> ¼ cup brown sugar
> ½ cup chopped walnuts
> ½ cup butter or margarine, melted
> 2 egg whites
> 1 cup granulated sugar
> 2 cups sliced fresh strawberries*
> 2 tablespoons lemon juice
> 1 cup whipping cream

Stir together first 4 ingredients; spread evenly in shallow baking pan. Bake at 350° for 20 minutes; stir occasionally. Sprinkle ⅔ *of the crumbs* in 13x9x2-inch baking pan.

Combine egg whites, granulated sugar, berries, and lemon juice in large bowl. With electric mixer beat at high speed to stiff peaks, about 10 minutes. Whip cream; fold into berry mixture. Spoon over crumbs; top with remaining crumbs. Freeze 6 hours or overnight. Cut in squares. Trim with whole strawberries, if desired. Makes 10 to 12 servings.

*Or use one 10-ounce package frozen strawberries, partially thawed (undrained); reduce granulated sugar to ⅔ cup.

Pastry desserts: No doubt, pie is the all-American dessert. Prepared with a variety of fillings, pastry-filled desserts range from the light and airy chiffons to the more robust fruit or frozen ice cream pies. Cream-filled pies topped with meringue and custard-type pies are additional favorites. Pastry is also used for cobblers, tarts, turnovers, and dumplings.

Puff pastry, unlike pastry for pies, produces a rich, flaky dough which expands greatly as it bakes. Napoleons are made from puff pastry. The pastry is baked, then separated into layers and spread with a custard-type filling. The pastry layers are reassembled to complete the dessert. Turnovers and Danish kringle are also prepared from puff pastry.

Brazilian Pie

> ⅓ cup sugar
> 1 envelope unflavored gelatin
>   (1 tablespoon)
> 1 tablespoon instant coffee
>   powder
> ¼ teaspoon ground nutmeg
>   Dash salt
> 3 slightly beaten egg yolks
> 1 14½-ounce can evaporated
>   milk (1⅔ cups)
> ½ teaspoon vanilla
>   • • •
> 3 egg whites
> ⅓ cup sugar
> 1 *baked* 9-inch pastry shell,
>   cooled
>   • • •
> ½ cup whipping cream
> 3 tablespoons grated unsweetened
>   chocolate

In saucepan combine first 5 ingredients. In bowl combine beaten egg yolks and evaporated milk. Add to gelatin mixture. Cook and stir till gelatin dissolves and mixture thickens slightly. Stir in vanilla. Chill, stirring occasionally, till partially set. Beat smooth.

Beat egg whites till soft peaks form. Gradually add ⅓ cup sugar, beating to stiff peaks. Fold in gelatin mixture. Pile into pastry shell. Chill till firm. To serve, whip cream. Spread atop pie; sprinkle with grated chocolate.

Mile High Ice Cream Pie

  1½ cups sifted all-purpose flour
  ½ teaspoon salt
  ½ cup shortening
  4 to 5 tablespoons cold water

      • • •

  1 pint vanilla ice cream
  1 pint chocolate ice cream

      • • •

  3 egg whites
  ½ teaspoon vanilla
  ¼ teaspoon cream of tartar
  6 tablespoons sugar

      • • •

  4 1-ounce squares unsweetened
     chocolate
  ¾ cup water
  1 cup sugar
    Dash salt
  6 tablespoons butter or margarine
  1 teaspoon vanilla

To prepare pastry, sift together flour and ½ teaspoon salt; cut in shortening with pastry blender till pieces are the size of small peas. Sprinkle 1 tablespoon cold water over part of mixture. Gently toss with fork; push to side of bowl. Repeat with remaining 3 to 4 tablespoons cold water till all is moistened.

Form into a ball. On lightly floured surface, roll to ⅛-inch thickness. Fit pastry into 9-inch pie plate; trim to 1 inch beyond edge. Fold edge under and flute. Prick bottom and sides with fork. Bake at 450° till golden, about 10 to 12 minutes. Cool pastry shell.

In cooled pie shell, layer vanilla ice cream, then chocolate ice cream.

To prepare meringue, beat egg whites with ½ teaspoon vanilla and cream of tartar till soft peaks form. Gradually add 6 tablespoons sugar, beating till stiff and glossy and sugar is dissolved. Spread meringue over ice cream, carefully sealing to edges of pastry. Bake at 475° till golden, about 4 to 5 minutes. Freeze pie several hours or overnight.

To prepare sauce, heat chocolate and ¾ cup water together over low heat, stirring constantly till melted and smooth. Stir in 1 cup sugar and dash salt; simmer till slightly thickened, about 5 minutes. Remove from heat; blend in butter and 1 teaspoon vanilla.

To serve, slice pie in wedges. Drizzle warm chocolate sauce over each serving.

Serving desserts

Always serve desserts attractively regardless of the occasion. With a little imagination, a plain dessert can often glamorize a meal for guests. You as a hostess will be much more at ease serving guests a favorite family dessert than if you prepare an unfamiliar dessert just because it may appear more elegant. For example, a simple fruit cup becomes a sophisticated dessert served in hollowed-out orange shells. And a simple fruit mixture is transformed into a flaming delight when served up in a chafing dish at the table. Likewise, individual tarts can replace the family's favorite pie for a company dessert.

Since dessert is served at the end of the meal, it is better to offer small helpings (with the invitation for seconds) than to serve too much to be enjoyed the first time around. Another important consideration for serving dessert is the temperature of the food. Some desserts are best served warm, while others should be eaten chilled; however, avoid extreme serving temperatures. Frozen desserts are best if allowed to stand at room temperature for a few minutes before they are served.

Desserts for mealtime: A well-planned menu includes a dessert compatible with the rest of the meal. Avoid repeating a food flavor which has already been served in the meal. Thus, if applesauce is served during the meal, it is better to select a dessert which doesn't include apples. Likewise, if two or more foods in the meal are accompanied with a sauce, plan a dessert which does not require a sauce.

The complexity of the meal determines to a great degree the type of dessert which is served. Many desserts can be prepared ahead of the meal so that more time can be devoted to the rest of the meal.

A simple dessert such as fruit or sherbet is an excellent way to end a heavy meal. Rich desserts are best served at the close of a light meal. Furthermore, respect for special diets and religious observances followed by family members or guests should be considered when planning the menu. Thus, dessert is a part of the total menu and provides a pleasant ending to the meal.

❧MENU❧

SATURDAY LUNCH
Grilled Reuben Sandwiches
Potato Chips
Celery and Carrot Sticks
Baked Ambrosia or *Hawaiian Fruit Crumble*
Coffee　　　　　　　　*Milk*

❧MENU❧

HAM DINNER
Broiled Ham Slice
Creamed Peas and New Potatoes
Fresh Fruit Salad
Fast Crème Brûlée
Coffee　　　　　　　　*Milk*

Baked Ambrosia

- 1 16-ounce can apricot halves
- 1 16-ounce can peach halves
- 1 16-ounce can purple plums
- 3 or 4 thin orange slices, halved
- ½ cup orange juice
- ¼ cup brown sugar
- ½ teaspoon shredded lemon peel
- 2 tablespoons butter or margarine, melted
- ½ cup flaked coconut

Thoroughly drain apricots, peaches, and plums. Arrange drained fruit with orange slices in a shallow baking dish. In small bowl combine orange juice, brown sugar, and shredded lemon peel; pour mixture over fruit.

Drizzle melted butter or margarine over plums; sprinkle flaked coconut over all fruit. Bake at 425° till hot and coconut is toasted, about 15 minutes. Serve warm. Serves 8.

Hawaiian Fruit Crumble

Toss 2 cups sliced, peeled tart apples with 1 tablespoon lemon juice; place in 10x6x1¾-inch baking dish. Spoon one 8¾-ounce can crushed pineapple, drained (¾ cup), evenly over apples; spread one 16-ounce can whole cranberry sauce (2 cups) atop pineapple.

For topping, mix 1 cup quick-cooking rolled oats, ¾ cup brown sugar, ½ cup all-purpose flour, ½ teaspoon ground cinnamon, and dash salt; cut in ⅓ cup butter or margarine till crumbly. Sprinkle crumb mixture over fruit. Bake at 350° till apples are tender, about 30 minutes. Serve warm. Makes 6 servings.

Fast Crème Brûlée

- 1 3- or 3¼-ounce package *regular* vanilla pudding mix
- ½ cup whipping cream
- ½ cup brown sugar

Prepare pudding mix according to package directions, *except use 1¾ cups milk*. Cool.

Whip cream. Fold into cooled pudding. Pour mixture into 9-inch pie plate. Chill.

Sprinkle brown sugar evenly over top. Place pie plate in shallow pan. Surround with ice cubes and a little cold water; broil 5 inches from heat till bubbly brown crust forms on top, about 5 minutes. Chill. Serves 4 to 6.

Desserts for entertaining: Elegant and sophisticated desserts are often served when entertaining guests. These desserts may involve more preparation but should still complement the rest of the meal.

Contemporary entertaining, however, may not involve a complete meal. Thus, desserts are a popular refreshment for such occasions. More elaborate desserts which may require last-minute preparation are possible since the hostess is not involved with the preparation of a meal.

Tortes, cheesecakes, shortcakes, parfaits, éclairs, Napoleons, baked Alaskas, soufflés, dessert pancakes, and cream puffs make impressive desserts for special occasions. For a large group, an assortment of desserts may be offered buffet style. Often very rich, these desserts are best served in small portions and accompanied by coffee, tea, or other suitable beverages.

Chocolate-Pecan Cornucopias

      2 sticks piecrust mix
    ¼ cup sugar
      1 tablespoon instant coffee
          powder
      1 cup whipping cream
    ½ cup grated sweet cooking
          chocolate
    ⅓ cup chopped pecans
          Pecan halves

Prepare pastry according to package directions. Roll to a 16x12-inch rectangle; cut into twelve 4-inch squares with pastry wheel. Roll each square to form a cone. For each pastry cone, fold a paper towel in quarters; shape into a cone. Insert paper cone in each pastry cone. Place on baking sheet; bake at 425° till golden brown, about 12 minutes. Remove paper toweling; cool cornucopias on rack.

Meanwhile, combine sugar, coffee powder, dash salt, and a little of the cream; stir till blended. Add remaining cream; chill. Whip till almost stiff. Fold in chocolate and chopped pecans. Spoon mixture into cornucopias; garnish with pecan halves. Makes 12 servings.

Heavenly Torte

      1 7-ounce jar marshmallow creme
      1 tablespoon hot water
    1½ teaspoons instant coffee powder
      1 teaspoon vanilla
      1 cup whipping cream
              • • •
      1 10-inch angel cake
    ½ 1-ounce square semisweet
          chocolate, shaved (3 tablespoons)
      2 tablespoons slivered almonds,
          toasted*

In small mixer bowl combine marshmallow creme, hot water, coffee powder, and vanilla. Beat at low speed of electric mixer till blended, then beat at high speed till fluffy.

Whip cream till soft peaks form. Fold whipped cream into marshmallow mixture.

Slice angel cake crosswise into three layers. Frost top of each layer with ⅓ of the marshmallow filling, then sprinkle with ⅓ of the shaved chocolate. Assemble frosted layers on cake plate; garnish top with toasted almonds.

*To toast, spread almonds on cookie sheet. Bake at 325° for 15 minutes; stir occasionally.

Chocolate-Pecan Cornucopias make a sophisticated dessert for entertaining. Cut and shaped from pastry mix, cornucopia shells boast a rich, mocha filling flecked with pecans.

MENU

HOLIDAY DINNER
Standing Rib Roast
Oven-Browned Potatoes   Brussels Sprouts
Molded Cranberry Salad
Brown-and-Serve Dinner Rolls   Butter
Lemon Angel Torte
Coffee

MENU

COMPANY DINNER
Broiled T-Bone Steaks
Baked Potatoes with Sour Cream
Tossed Green Salad
Garlic Bread
Cherries Portofino or Company Cheesecake
Coffee

Lemon Angel Torte

4 egg whites
¼ teaspoon cream of tartar
¾ cup sugar

• • •

4 egg yolks
1 tablespoon grated lemon peel
3 tablespoons lemon juice
½ cup sugar

• • •

1 cup whipping cream

For shell: Preheat oven to 450°. Beat whites with electric mixer till foamy; add cream of tartar and ¼ teaspoon salt. Slowly add ¾ cup sugar; beat to stiff peaks, about 7 minutes. Spread in buttered 9-inch pie plate, forming edge. Place in preheated oven; turn off heat. Let stand in *closed* oven 4 hours or overnight.

For filling: In top of double boiler beat egg yolks till thick and lemon-colored. Gradually beat in lemon peel, lemon juice, ½ cup sugar, and dash salt. Cook and stir over gently boiling water till thick, about 8 minutes. Remove from heat; cover and cool.

To assemble: Whip cream. Spread *half* of the whipped cream in shell; cover with filling. Top with remaining whipped cream, covering edges. Wrap loosely; chill 3 hours or overnight.

Easy and elegant

← Creamy coffee-flavored filling dotted with shaved chocolate oozes from between layers of angel cake in Heavenly Torte dessert.

Cherries Portofino

1 16-ounce can pitted dark sweet cherries
½ cup port
2 3-ounce packages raspberry-flavored gelatin
2 cups boiling water
1 quart vanilla ice cream, softened

Drain cherries, reserving syrup. Combine drained cherries and wine; let stand 3 hours.

Dissolve gelatin in boiling water. Drain cherries, reserving wine. Combine wine with reserved cherry juice and enough cold water to make 1½ cups. Stir into dissolved gelatin. Chill till partially set. Stir in cherries. Pour into 11¾x7½x1¾-inch dish. Chill till firm.

To serve, cut into cubes; spoon into sherbet glasses. Top with ice cream. Serves 8.

Company Cheesecake

Combine 1¾ cups fine graham cracker crumbs; ¼ cup finely chopped walnuts; ½ teaspoon ground cinnamon; and ½ cup butter or margarine, melted. Press on bottom and ⅔ of the way up sides of 9-inch springform pan.

Combine 3 well-beaten eggs; two 8-ounce packages cream cheese, softened; 1 cup sugar; ¼ teaspoon salt; 2 teaspoons vanilla; and ¼ teaspoon almond extract. Beat till smooth.

Blend in 3 cups dairy sour cream. Pour into crust. Bake at 375° till set, about 35 minutes; cool. Chill 4 to 5 hours. (Filling will be soft.) Makes 12 to 16 servings.

DESSERT SAUCE—A thickened sauce, usually sweetened, that tops a dessert.

Dessert sauces can spark a wide array of dessert foods by providing the extra touch that turns an ordinary dessert into a dazzling delight. Ice creams and sherbets, pies, cakes, and fruits or fruit-based desserts are frequently dressed up with a sauce. In fact, an intriguing sauce served over a simple base, such as vanilla ice cream or yellow cake, often develops into the star course of a menu.

The most common dessert foods served with a sauce are ice cream and sherbet. Often a spectacular display is created by spooning flaming sauces over each portion. Chocolate or fruit-filled sauces can be the beginnings for rich ice cream sundaes and multi-layered parfaits.

Cakes, particularly when unfrosted, and pies can also be glamorized with the addition of a sauce. Cake that has started to dry is revived to moistening goodness by spooning a sauce over each slice. A luscious fruit sauce with a dollop of whipped cream atop is an attractive finish to a serving of light lemon chiffon pie.

Don't forget the easy way to brighten fruit desserts either. A thick custard or lemon sauce transforms a fresh fruit cup finale into a rare treat. Lemon and custard sauces are also traditional crowning touches for fruit-filled steamed puddings and oven-fresh cottage puddings.

Sauces not only give desserts a more glamorous touch but also are a quick and convenient way to create a last-minute refreshment. Many sauces are prepared in advance, then stored in the refrigerator. These sauces are then served right from the refrigerator; a quick reheating brings the sauces back to their original delicious state. (See also *Sauce*.)

Marshmallow Sauce

    ½ 1-pint jar marshmallow creme
    ¼ cup pineapple juice

Spoon marshmallow creme into small mixer bowl. Gradually add pineapple juice, beating at high speed of electric mixer till thickened, about 5 minutes. Makes 1 cup.

Golden Raisin Flambé

A chafing dish specialty that's easy to fix, yet decidedly glamorous and delicious—

    ½ cup light raisins
        • • •
    ¼ cup brandy
    3 tablespoons brown sugar
    ¼ teaspoon grated lemon peel
    1 tablespoon lemon juice
        • • •
    ¼ cup brandy
        Vanilla ice cream

In saucepan cover raisins with water. Bring to boiling; simmer 5 minutes. Drain. Add the first ¼ cup brandy, brown sugar, lemon peel, and lemon juice. Cover; let stand at least 1 hour.

At serving time transfer raisin mixture to blazer pan of small chafing dish. Bring to boiling over direct heat. In small saucepan heat remaining ¼ cup brandy. Ignite; spoon over sauce. Serve raisin sauce over vanilla ice cream. Makes 6 servings.

Melted peppermint-flavored marshmallows impart a creamy smoothness and refreshing flavor to Mallow-Mint Sauce.

Mallow-Mint Sauce

 3 cups peppermint-flavored marsh-
     mallows (29 marshmallows)
 1 tablespoon butter or margarine
 1 6-ounce can evaporated milk
     ($\frac{2}{3}$ cup)
 $\frac{1}{4}$ teaspoon vanilla
 2 or 3 drops red food coloring
   Vanilla ice cream

In top of double boiler combine marshmallows, butter, and $\frac{1}{4}$ *cup* of the evaporated milk. Cook and stir over hot water till marshmallows melt and mixture is smooth; remove from heat. Stir in remaining evaporated milk, vanilla, and red food coloring; mix well. Serve sauce warm over vanilla ice cream. Garnish with mint sprigs, if desired. Makes $1\frac{1}{4}$ cups.

Candied Ginger Sauce

 $\frac{1}{2}$ cup sugar
 $\frac{1}{4}$ cup orange-flavored breakfast
     drink powder
 2 tablespoons cornstarch
 2 tablespoons finely snipped
     candied ginger
   Dash salt
 $1\frac{1}{2}$ cups water
 2 tablespoons butter or margarine

In saucepan combine sugar, drink powder, cornstarch, candied ginger, and salt. Gradually stir in water, blending well. Bring to boiling; boil for 2 minutes, stirring constantly. Remove from heat. Blend in butter or margarine; cool. (If refrigerated, stir sauce well before serving.) Makes $1\frac{3}{4}$ cups.

Golden Apricot Sauce

 1 30-ounce can apricot halves
 $\frac{3}{4}$ cup sugar
 $\frac{1}{4}$ cup orange juice
 $\frac{1}{2}$ teaspoon almond extract

Drain apricots, reserving $\frac{1}{2}$ cup syrup. Cut up apricots and stir in reserved syrup, sugar, orange juice, and dash salt. Simmer 10 minutes, stirring occasionally. Stir in extract; chill. Serve over ice cream. Makes 2 cups.

Cherry Sauce

 $\frac{3}{4}$ cup sugar
 2 tablespoons cornstarch
   Dash salt
 1 20-ounce can pitted tart
     red cherries, undrained
 10 drops red food coloring

Combine sugar, cornstarch, and salt. Stir in undrained cherries. Cook quickly, stirring constantly, till mixture is thickened and bubbly. Reduce heat; cook 1 minute more. Add food coloring. Serve warm. Makes $2\frac{3}{4}$ cups.

Mocha Sauce

 1 cup sugar
 $\frac{1}{3}$ cup unsweetened cocoa powder
 1 tablespoon cornstarch
 1 tablespoon instant coffee powder
       • • •
 1 $14\frac{1}{2}$-ounce can evaporated milk
 $\frac{1}{4}$ teaspoon vanilla
   Vanilla ice cream

In saucepan combine sugar, cocoa, cornstarch, and coffee powder. Gradually stir in milk. Cook, stirring constantly, till mixture is thickened and bubbly. Remove from heat; stir in vanilla. Spoon over ice cream. Makes 6 servings.

Nutmeg-Pineapple Sauce

 $\frac{1}{2}$ cup granulated sugar
 $\frac{1}{2}$ cup brown sugar
 $\frac{1}{2}$ cup light corn syrup
 $\frac{1}{4}$ cup butter or margarine
 $\frac{1}{2}$ teaspoon ground nutmeg
       • • •
 1 $13\frac{1}{2}$-ounce can pineapple
     tidbits, drained
 $\frac{1}{4}$ teaspoon vanilla
 10 slices sponge cake, angel cake,
     pound cake, *or* vanilla
     ice cream

In saucepan combine granulated sugar, brown sugar, corn syrup, butter, and nutmeg. Cook, stirring constantly, till mixture boils. Stir in pineapple and vanilla. Spoon hot pineapple sauce over cake or ice cream. Makes 10 servings.

Quick Fudge Sauce

    1 6-ounce package semisweet
        chocolate pieces (1 cup)
    1 6-ounce can evaporated milk
        (⅔ cup)
    ½ 1-pint jar marshmallow creme

In saucepan combine chocolate pieces and
evaporated milk. Cook and stir over low heat
till well combined. Beat in marshmallow creme
till mixture is thoroughly blended. Serve warm
or cool. Makes 2 cups.

Peanut Butter–Marshmallow Sauce

    1 5½-ounce package peanut butter
        pieces (1 cup)
    ½ cup light cream
    ½ cup miniature marshmallows
    1 teaspoon vanilla
      Toasted coconut

Melt peanut butter pieces in light cream over
low heat, stirring constantly. Add marshmallows, stirring till melted. Remove from heat;
add vanilla. Serve warm or chilled. Top each
serving with coconut. Makes 1½ cups.

Creamy Butterscotch Sauce

    ½ cup butter or margarine
    2 cups brown sugar
    1 cup light corn syrup
    1 15-ounce can sweetened
        condensed milk (1⅓ cups)
    1 teaspoon vanilla

In saucepan melt butter; stir in sugar, corn
syrup, and 2 tablespoons water. Bring to boiling. Stir in milk; simmer, stirring constantly,
till mixture reaches thread stage (230°). Add
vanilla. Serve warm over ice cream or cake.

DESSERT TOPPING—A light, fluffy foam
whipped from a dairy or non-dairy base
and used like whipped cream. Dessert toppings may be purchased in several forms:
in the prewhipped and frozen state, in
aerosol cans, as a dry mix, or as a liquid.
The first two types require no pre-prepa-
ration. The dry mix, on the other hand,
must be combined with milk prior to whipping, while the liquid dessert topping is
simply whipped to soft peaks.

Dessert toppings have gained consider-
ably in popularity because they are low in
cost. Many maintain a stable foam for
many days when refrigerated. And others
are pleasingly light in calorie content.

Banana Split Pie

    3 medium bananas
    1 tablespoon lemon juice
    1 9-inch *baked* pastry shell, cooled
        (see *Pastry*)
    1 pint strawberry ice cream
        • • •
    1 cup frozen whipped dessert
        topping, thawed
      Whole maraschino cherries
    2 tablespoons finely chopped
        walnuts
      Canned chocolate sauce

Thinly slice bananas; sprinkle with lemon
juice and arrange on bottom of baked pastry
shell. Stir strawberry ice cream to soften slightly; spread atop bananas. Freeze till firm.
Spread dessert topping over ice cream. Top
with cherries; sprinkle with nuts. Freeze firm.

Let frozen pie stand 30 minutes at room
temperature before serving. Spoon canned
chocolate sauce over each serving.

Mocha-Velvet Torte

    1 12-ounce loaf pound cake
    1 4½-ounce package *instant*
        chocolate pudding mix
    1 2-ounce package dessert topping
        mix
    1 tablespoon instant coffee powder
    1¼ cups cold milk

Slice cake horizontally in 4 layers. For frosting
combine pudding mix, dessert topping mix, instant coffee powder, and milk in mixing bowl.
Beat till fluffy and of spreading consistency.
Spread three layers of cake with frosting; stack
together and top with fourth layer. Frost top
and sides of cake. Chill. Serves 10.